RAMBLE
LEEDS

Volume 1 : East of Leeds

25 MOSTLY CIRCULAR WALKS WITH SKETCH MAPS

Compiled by

Douglas Cossar

for the Ramblers' Association (West Riding Area)

The Ramblers

Other publications by the Ramblers' Association (West Riding Area)

Kiddiwalks
Douglas Cossar, *The Airedale Way*
Douglas Cossar, *Ramblers' Wakefield*
Marje Wilson, *The Brontë Way*
Dales Way Handbook (with the Dales Way Association, annually)
Douglas Cossar, *Ramblers' Bradford* (autumn 1999)

Ramblers' Leeds first published 1995

2nd revised and expanded edition in two volumes 1999

RAMBLERS' ASSOCIATION (WEST RIDING AREA)
27 Cookridge Avenue, Leeds LS16 7NA

ISBN 1 901184 23 4

Front cover photograph: Link path from Trans Pennine Trail to Leeds Country Way at Swillington Bridge. *Rear cover photographs:* Footpath by Wharfe east of Collingham Church, Aire & Calder Navigation near Woodlesford Lock, Temple Newsam Bridleway looking south from Dog Kennel Hill. All photographs © Leeds City Council, taken by R.Brookes.

Publishers' Note
At the time of publication all footpaths used in these walks were designated as public rights of way or permissive footpaths, but it should be borne in mind that diversion orders may be made from time to time. Although every care has been taken in the preparation of this guide, neither the author nor the publisher can accept responsibility for those who stray from the routes described.

In affectionate memory of

Eric Barker
(1924-1997)

a tireless defender of
the footpaths of Leeds

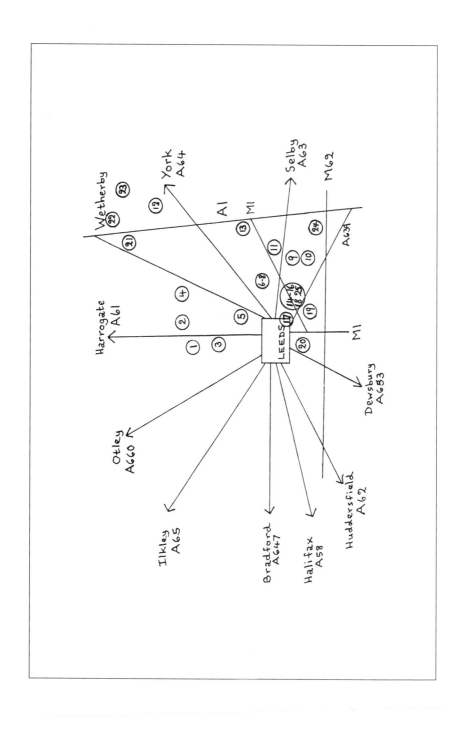

Contents

The **Ramblers' Association,** a registered charity, is an organisation dedicated to the preservation and care of the countryside and its network of footpaths, and to helping people to appreciate and enjoy them.

Through its Central Office the Ramblers' Association lobbies and campaigns for more effective legislation to achieve

- the preservation and improvement of the footpath network

- better access to the countryside

- the preservation and enhancement for the benefit of the public of the beauty of the countryside.

Since its formation in 1935 the Ramblers' Association has grown into a powerful campaigning organisation with a membership of 125,000.

The Association relies on many volunteers working at Area and Local Group level to help achieve these objectives.

The **West Riding Area** is one of the 51 Areas of the Ramblers' Association which cover England, Wales and Scotland. It includes the whole of West Yorkshire and parts of North Yorkshire around Selby, York, Harrogate, Ripon, Skipton and Settle, as well as the southern part of the Yorkshire Dales National Park. The Area has over 4,000 members and is divided into 13 Local Groups.

The **Local Groups** carry out the work of the Ramblers' Association by keeping an eye on the state of footpaths in their area and monitoring proposed closures and diversions.

- They put pressure on their Local Authority to take action to remove obstructions and re-instate footpaths after ploughing.

- They do practical work of footpath clearance and waymarking, and can erect stiles and footbridges.

- Where the Local Authority has set up consultation procedures, e.g. Footpath Forums, the Local Group will normally send a representative.

- Many Local Groups produce their own programme of walks.

Regular walks are a very important part of Ramblers' activities. As well as ensuring that local footpaths are used, they provide healthy recreation and the opportunity to make new friends.

If you use and enjoy the footpath network, please help us to protect it, by joining the Ramblers' Association. For further information write to the West Riding Area Membership Secretary

Mrs Dora Tattersall, 2 Southend, Raines Road, Giggleswick, Settle BD24 0BW, or to

The Ramblers' Association, 1/5 Wandsworth Road, London SW8 2XX.

Author's note

Since *Ramblers' Leeds* first appeared in the spring of 1995 many changes have taken place which have affected local footpaths, not least the opening of the A1-M1 link and the consequent upgrading of the A1 between Micklefield and the A64 to motorway status. I have therefore taken the opportunity to make a complete revision of the earlier volume, to add some new walks, and to split the book into two parts, the first to cover very roughly the area east of the city of Leeds, the second that to the west.

In this first volume, Walks 1-20 are the same as Walks 1-20 of the first edition, while Walks 21-25 are new.

Leeds in the context of this book means the Metropolitan District of Leeds, and a substantial part of the route of each walk is within the Leeds District, although I have allowed myself to stray over the border from time to time for the sake of a more interesting ramble. I have tried to achieve a wide geographical spread of walks, and I hope that on the whole the two parts of *Ramblers' Leeds* represent reasonably well the variety and interest of the landscapes of Leeds. Those of us who live in and around the city have much to be grateful for.

All the paths used are definitive rights of way or permissive footpaths, and they are on the whole in good shape, thanks both to the vigilance and pressure of the Ramblers' Association and to the committed attitude of Leeds Leisure Services Public Rights of Way Section. If you should encounter any obstacles, obstructions, nuisances or other difficulties, please report them, either to the Footpaths Officer of the Leeds Group of the RA, Alan Beal, 433 Oakwood Lane, Leeds LS8 3LF (Tel.:0113-240-2615), or to Leeds City Council's Rights of Way Section at Red Hall, Red Hall Lane, Leeds LS17 8NB (Tel: 0113-232-9422). As a result of recent tragic accidents, dogs now seem generally to be kept under much better control than formerly, but do look out for bulls at large in pastures in the summer months, and take suitable evasive action, even if this means a minor trespass. Better safe than sorry!

I am again most grateful to Roger Brookes of the Rights of Way Section for giving me his time and the benefit of his knowledge of local footpath developments and for suggesting corrections and improvements to my routes. The final responsibility for the walks is of course my own.

All the walks can be located on the Ordnance Survey Landranger maps 104 (Leeds & Bradford, Harrogate & Ilkley) and 105 (York), and at the start of each walk I have given details of the relevant Pathfinder sheet(s). The new Leeds & Selby Explorer map, due out by the end of 2000, will replace several local Pathfinders. The sketch maps which accompany each walk are based on these Pathfinder maps and are reproduced with the permission of the Controller of H.M.S.O. They are intended to give an overview of the walk and to supplement the description, but as they are greatly simplified, particularly in built-up areas, **they should not be used as a substitute for the description.** Please read the descriptions carefully: I have tried to make them clear and unambiguous and to eliminate the risk of misinterpretation. I am sure you will let me know where I have failed! But in my experience lots of people go astray through not concentrating on the text of a walk, inadvertently skipping a line or jumping by mistake from one stile to the next, or just losing the place through being engrossed in conversation with their companions!

All the walks are accessible by public transport, and I have given details as they are known to me at the moment. But please do check this information with West Yorkshire Metro (Tel: 0113-245-7676).

I should like to dedicate this volume to the memory of Eric Barker, whose knowledge of the footpaths of the Leeds area was encyclopaedic and who for many years was deeply involved in their preservation and protection. Eric was one of my heroes when I first became active in footpath work for the Ramblers' Association, and I am proud to have been given this chance to produce a tribute to his achievements.

Douglas Cossar
May 1999

Remember the Country Code:

Guard against all risk of fire.

Take your litter home. As well as being unsightly, it may be a hazard to livestock.

If you find a gate closed, be careful to close it again behind you. If it is open, leave it open.

Do not pollute streams or rivers, ponds, lakes or reservoirs.

Keep dogs under control: they may frighten other walkers or be a threat to livestock.

Protect, wildlife, plants and trees.

Keep to public paths across farmland.

Take special care on country roads.

Use gates and stiles to cross fences, hedges and walls.

Make no unnecessary noise.

Leave livestock, crops and machinery alone.

Enjoy the countryside and respect its life and work.

HAREWOOD CIRCULAR

WALK 1

6½ miles (10¼ km); Pathfinder 672; an easy ramble almost entirely on tracks, partly through the parkland and woods of the Harewood Estate.

By bus: No. 36/36A Leeds-Harrogate-Ripon bus (every 20 minutes at 15, 35 and 55 minutes past the hour, hourly evenings and Sundays) from Leeds Central Bus Station. Alight at a gate on the left into the Harewood Estate, opposite a minor road to Wike on the right.

By car: Coming from Leeds on the A61 to Harrogate, shortly after the wall enclosing the Harewood estate begins on the left, there is a large wrought iron gate into the estate by a lodge, and opposite there is a minor road signposted to Wike. A few yards along this road there is a large layby with a memorial seat. Park here (GR 326 432) and return to and cross the main road.

Go through the right hand of the three large gates and head along the track through the park. Immediately there is a fine view right to Harewood House and Lower Wharfedale. Pass through another two gates, and the track is now gently descending. Go through another gate and into the wood. Cross an 18th century stone bridge and bear left (bridleway sign). At the next fork keep right (signpost: you will note that you are on the Leeds Country Way). Shortly before you reach the end of the wood, with fields ahead, fork right at a junction of tracks (signpost) and cross the shallow valley of Stub House Beck. The buildings over to the left are the set for YTV's "Emmerdale Farm". At the next crossing fork right (Ebor Way sign) on a descending track, soon coming to a T-junction where again you bear right downhill.

The track leads to a gate into a field, but 200 yards before this, fork left onto another descending track, which leads to the left of a stone barn. Pass through the gate and keep forward down the track. The lake and the house are seen in the distance. Bear left at the next junction, and the track soon curves right to a gate. Pass to the left of an old walled garden. You are joined by a tarmac track from the right, and soon there is a fine view over Wharfedale to Weeton and Almscliff Crag. Drop to a crossroads: a short distance over the bridge on the right is Harewood House, but there is no right of way to it. Keep forward over another bridge then uphill through the Home Farm, now converted into offices.

Cross a cattle-grid to re-enter the park. Cross another cattle-grid and walk forward to a junction (another nice view), where you bear right uphill. Cross another cattle-grid. The track on the right at this point leads to the mediaeval Harewood Parish Church, open every afternoon in summer and worth a visit, but our walk continues straight ahead to Harewood village. Keep forward to the main road, cross it (care!) and turn right, but only as far as the Harewood Arms. Immediately before the pub take the signposted path on the left, a tarmac lane. At the gate into Maltkiln House the lane bears slightly right, and when the tarmac ends go

9

through the gate ahead and keep forward along the track with a small wood to the right (another fine view left over Wharfedale). Cross the stile by the next gate and immediately go right over a stile and walk down the right hand edge of the field to the A659 Harewood to Wetherby road.

Turn left along the road (there is a narrow footway). Shortly after passing a long layby and opposite a milepost take the access road on the right to New Laithe Farm. When the road forks just before the farm, keep left and pass round the left hand end of the farmhouse onto a concrete track, and when this ends keep straight forward downhill with a hedge to your right to another gate. Keep forward down the next large field to a gate near the left hand end of a row of tall trees. The gate is quickly followed by another one, and now you must bear slightly left uphill (no clear path) to the left hand end of the buildings of Hollin Hall ahead. Pass to the left of the house, through a gate and straight downhill on a track to pass to the left of a lake. When you reach the wood bear right up to a gateway, then left on the track along the outside edge of the wood.

The track soon bears slightly right uphill away from the wood, and when it peters out keep forward to a gate in the top left hand corner of the field. Now there is a clear track again, up with the hedge to your left. Enter a hedged track and follow it up to a T-junction with a Leeds Country Way signpost, where you turn right along the track. When it forks, keep right, i.e. straight on, soon passing to the left of Wike Wood. At the motor road turn right to return to the starting point.

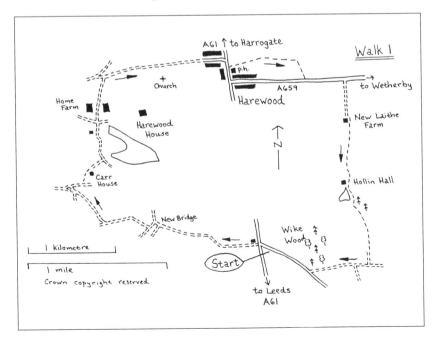

RIVER WHARFE, KEARBY, WOODHALL BRIDGE AND CARTHICK WOOD

WALK 2

8½ miles (13¾ km); Pathfinder 672. The intention is to walk upstream from Woodhall Bridge along the south bank of the Wharfe as far as the next river crossing at Harewood Bridge, returning along the opposite bank, but the layout of the rights of way means that the walk has much more variety than a purely riverside ramble. Lovely pastoral countryside with attractive views. The outward leg coincides with the Ebor Way.

By bus: No. 98/99 Leeds – Wetherby half-hourly, hourly evenings and Sundays from Leeds Infirmary Street, Headrow, Eastgate. Alight at junction of Crabtree Lane and the A659 Harewood – Wetherby road on the edge of East Keswick.

By car: Park in the large layby with picnic table at the junction of Crabtree Lane and the A659 Harewood – Wetherby road on the outskirts of East Keswick (GR 362 454).

Cross the busy main road and turn left along it for about a quarter of a mile. This is unpleasant, because the traffic is fast and for much of the way there is no verge to walk on, but there are pleasant views over Wharfedale. At the top of a slight rise, 40 yards before a minor road forks left, take the signposted path on the right over a stile by the left hand gate and walk down the field to the next stile in a few yards. Now continue down close to the right hand edge of the field. There is an old hollow way, but so overgrown that it is easier to keep to the left of it. Soon a clear path bears right through the line of trees and drops straight down the slope, passing through a gateway to reach a stile by a gate. Cross, and the river is below. Bear left with the path downhill.

Soon bear right into a field and keep forward along the riverbank. Shortly there is a narrow wood between you and the river: do not be tempted to enter this wood, but keep along the righthand edge of the large field. And don't be diverted left at an old field boundary: keep on with the wood to your right. Soon after the wood ends you are once more close to the river. A little further and you again have a wood to the right. About 200 yards before the facing wood at the end of this field turn right on a waymarked path (be careful not to miss it) into Carthick Wood and follow the clear narrow path, which can be overgrown in summer, as it soon bears left and reaches the riverbank. Turn left along by the river. Leave the wood by a stile and continue along the righthand edge of the field.

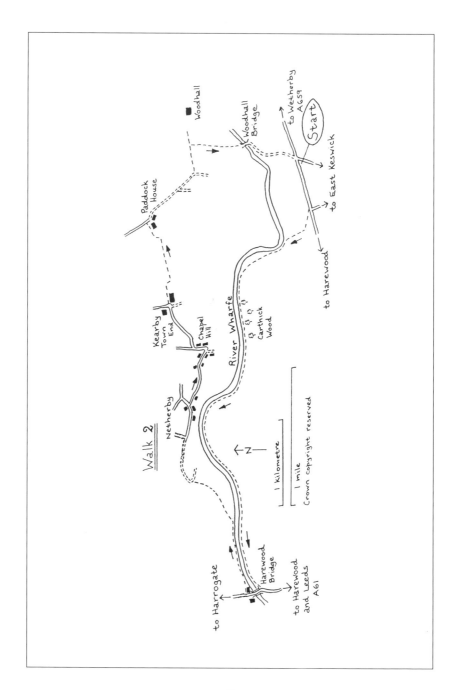

Walk 2

Woodhall

Paddock House

Kearby Town End

Chapel Hill

Netherby

River Wharfe

Carthick Wood

Woodhall Bridge

to Wetherby A659

Start

to East Keswick

to Harewood

N

1 kilometre

1 mile

Crown copyright reserved

to Harrogate

Harewood Bridge

to Harewood and Leeds A61

12

Now essentially you follow the riverbank all the way to Harewood Bridge, at first along the flood embankment. After leaving the embankment follow the good track forward, but when this bears left uphill towards Harewood village, cross a stile and keep forward along the riverbank, along the righthand edge of a field. Just before an old stone building which looks like some sort of chimney the path bears right out of the field to pass to the right of this structure and proceed forward to a stile by a gate into another enormous field. Follow the righthand edge of this field, with Harewood Bridge now drawing closer, and about 100 yards before the bridge look out for a path forking half-right out of the field and descending gently closer to the river. Follow this path along to a stile out onto the main road and turn right over the bridge. Here you leave the Ebor Way.

Immediately past the large house on the right turn right along a tarmac lane, and when the tarmac ends, keep forward along the track. Soon the river is close by on the right. After some time the track bears left and reaches a cross-track: turn right along it and shortly afterwards bear half-left with the track across a large field, away from the river. On approaching a hedge and a short length of wall across the line of the track, cross a little ditch and go through a small wooden gate in the wall. Keep along the lefthand edge of the next field until you meet a concrete track at a hairpin bend, where there is a wide bridge with metal side-rails. Turn left over the bridge and follow the hedged track to a right-angle bend on a tarmac road. Ignore the road to the left (Wharfe Lane) and keep straight on into Netherby, then take the first road on the right towards Kearby (Chapel Hill).

Follow the road uphill to this attractive hamlet, ignore a No Through Road forking right on the bend, and bear sharply left with the road uphill. At the top, just before the road junction, look left over the wall for a fine view up Wharfedale to Almscliff Crag. Then fork right along the road to Wetherby (Gill Lane). When you reach the houses at Kearby Town End the road bears left, and just round this bend there is a track forking right, passing to the left of Manor Farm, through the farmyard and into a hedged track. When the hedge on the left ends, keep with the track along the right hand edge of the field, bearing left in 100 yards with the track and hedge (ignoring the large gate on the right). Pass through a large gate and follow the fence on the left. At the end of this large field (you are high up and there is a fine view over Wharfedale), cross the stile and turn left with the fence to your left, soon bearing right with this fence to a stile in the far corner of the field. Cross this, then a farm track, and follow the fence on your left, to pass through a gap in the facing hedge onto Paddock House Lane.

Turn right down the lane, soon following it left past Paddock House. When the road forks, keep left, still on tarmac; there follows a straight stretch, with the road descending gently, and at the end of it there is a right hand bend: on this bend leave the tarmac and fork left through a gate on a track, which you follow towards an old walled garden in the distance. Ignore the gate in the wall ahead at the far side of the field and turn right down the track with the walled garden to your left (here re-joining the Ebor Way). Pass through two bridle-gates close together and follow the fenced path to Woodhall Bridge, where you re-cross the Wharfe. Bear right with the path, which can be muddy, (a stile by a bridle-gate on the left gives access to Ox Close Wood Nature Reserve) but soon the path becomes a track which climbs to the A659 and your starting point.

THE CIRCUIT OF ECCUP RESERVOIR

WALK 3

4¼ miles (7 km); Pathfinder 672. An easy pastoral stroll on clear paths, tracks and a minor road. The path by the reservoir is popular with joggers and twitchers!

By bus: No. 34/35 from Infirmary Street/Boar Lane/Vicar Lane/New Briggate every 15 minutes, hourly evenings and Sundays. Alight on Alwoodley Lane near its junction with The Avenue, and keeping The Avenue on your right walk along Alwoodley Lane for about 200 yards until you are opposite its junction with Mount Drive;

By car: Park on Alwoodley Lane near its junction with Lakeland Drive and opposite Mount Drive.

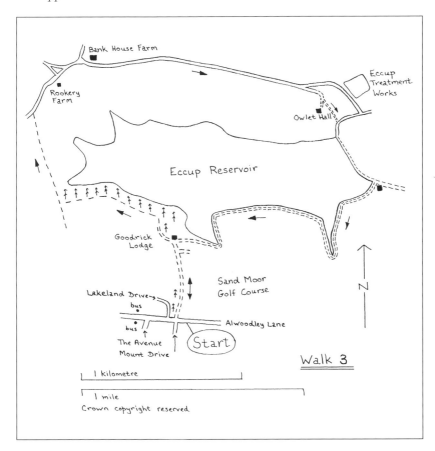

A public footpath sign points through large white gates along a tarmac drive with a No Entry sign. Follow this drive with a small conifer wood to the left and soon Sand Moor Golf Course to the right. At the foot of the hill, with Goodrick Lodge straight ahead and the reservoir visible to the right, turn left along the track. It leads to a gate: pass through and continue with the wood to your right, soon bearing left with the fence. Follow the fence all the way to a stile on the right at the far end of the wood (here you join the Dales Way Leeds-Ilkley Link), and then the path leads downhill to another stile. Keep forward up across the middle of the field, and towards the far side keep to the right of a hedge which you follow to another stile and a road.

Turn right along the road. In the bottom of a dip cross Eccup Beck and ignore another road forking left and at the top of the next rise a road coming in from the left. Just before Bank House Farm ignore a bridleway forking left (with the Dales Way Link) and follow the road past the farm and past a No Entry sign into a Yorkshire Water private road which is also a public bridleway.

Leave the road where a signposted bridleway forks right off it along a track. When the track bends right towards Owlet Hall Farm, go through a bridle-gate on the left and follow the fenced bridleway down to another tarmac road, on which you must turn right. The road bends left over the reservoir dam (here on the right by a pumping station there are picnic tables with a pleasant view over the reservoir). At the far side, just before the lodge, go through the kissing-gate on the right into a fenced track. Follow this all the way back to Goodrick Lodge and return up the tarmac road by your outward route to the starting point.

BARDSEY, HETCHELL CRAGS AND THORNER

WALK 4

7 miles (11¼ km); Pathfinder 672. A mix of woodland, arable and pasture, mainly on clear and easy paths. Part of the route is popular with horse-riders and can be muddy. The Hetchell Wood Nature Reserve merits a leisurely exploration: the route chosen here uses one of several possible paths.

By bus: No. 98, 99 Wetherby bus from Leeds Infirmary Street (half-hourly). Alight a few yards before the start of the 40 m.p.h. limit at Bardsey and walk back towards Leeds until you reach a large layby on the other side of the road.
By car: From Scarcroft the A58 Leeds to Wetherby road swings downhill to Bardsey. At the bottom of the hill, with a wood on the right, there is a large layby. Park here (GR 369 430).

Enter the wood through the bollards. The path soon joins the old railway track: bear right along it for a few yards, then fork left over a stile. The path soon follows the left hand edge of a grassy area with trees to the left, and where this ends keep forward along a clear path with a fence to your left and a hedge to your right. When the hedge bears right follow it, ignoring a clear path forward up the middle of the field. The hedge soon ends, and you keep along the bottom edge of the field with Bardsey Beck to your right. A stile leads into Hetchell Wood.

The path bears right and climbs gently through the wood, soon passing to the right of Hetchell Crags (ignore paths forking left here). When you reach stepping stones over the beck on your right, turn left, at first with a fence to your right, but soon passing through a kissing-gate onto a track. This track, an old Roman road, is a popular bridleway and can be muddy. The earthworks over the fence on the right are known as Pompocali. Follow the track up to a motor road, then cross diagonally left to a path on the right to a large gate. Pass round the gate and continue along the edge of the field with the remains of a hedge to your right. After a time the path enters woodland, keeping close to the left hand edge of the wood. Follow it to a signposted T-junction at the far end of the wood and turn right, in a few yards keeping left at a fork.

After a time the track descends gently and you reach another fork: the left branch is about to curve left, we bear right along a narrower path. In the valley to the left is Milner Beck. Eventually you turn right (signpost) and the path leads out of the woodland and up the left hand edge of a field. At the top the path turns left again as a broad track. In a few yards ignore a track forking right. Pass a barn and follow the track for about 1100 yards until you come to a wide gap in the hedge on the left. (It is not the first wide gap you come to, but the second, and it is signposted, and when you turn left through it, the hedge you are going to follow down leads slightly to the left of the right hand end of the wood on the other side of the valley, a wood which has fields to the right of it.) So turn through the gap and follow the clear path down with the hedge to your right. At the bottom of the field continue downhill through the wood to cross Thorner Beck by the Jubilee Bridge.

Bear right to a stile into a field and walk straight forward across the field, soon picking up a hedge to your right. Where the hedge ends keep forward to a stile, and now again there is a hedge/fence to your right. When the hedge kinks right and then left, keep forward to cut the corner of the field to a kissing-gate which leads down some steps onto a road. Turn left along the road into Thorner. When you reach a main road bear right towards the church. Directly opposite the church tower turn right down a ginnel, which soon bears right, crosses Mill Beck, then turns left under the old railway track. On reaching a tarmac road keep forward along it, and at the main motor road continue for a few yards further, then just before the footway starts turn right up a track.

At the end of the track go through two kissing-gates ahead and follow the hollow way with the hedge to your right. Where the hedge ends keep forward down the right hand edge of the field to a footbridge and kissing-gate at the bottom. Now the path bears very slightly left up the next long field to a stile in the fence on the left to the right of

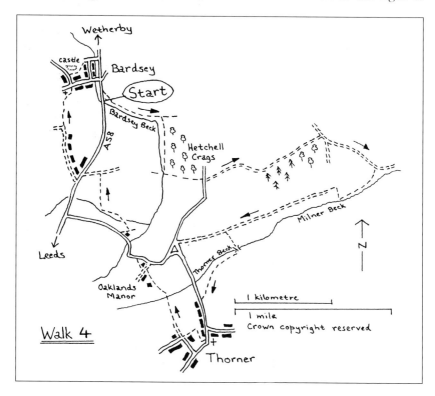

Oaklands Manor. Continue up the walled lane, and at the end go left along the tarmac lane. Immediately after a large barn on the right go through a small metal gate on the right and walk across the lefthand end of the concrete yard to two more small gates at the far end. Once in the field walk forward to the end of the buildings on the right, then bear half-right down the field to a double stile at the next road.

Turn left down the road. Cross Scarcroft Beck, and immediately after a large white house on the right turn right along a track signposted Scarcroft and Nature Reserve. Just after the second house cross the signposted stile on the left and follow the right hand edge of the field. The well-used path soon bears right to a stile, crosses a footbridge and in a few yards reaches a field where it bears left then left again along an old hedged lane. (Be careful not to keep along the field-edge at this point.) Follow the path until it leads into a field, then keep up the right hand edge of the field. Follow the hedge on the right to a cross-track and turn left along it, ignoring the track straight ahead and keeping an old wall to your right. Now we shall complete our round with a stroll to Bardsey Church and the site of the castle. (Bus passengers who wish to end the walk here can catch a bus back to Leeds from a stop a few yards to the left along the A58.)

When you reach the A58 cross it and go left for a few yards, there turning right into Wayside Mount, an unsurfaced no through road. After the houses end pass through the gate and keep forward on the track between fields, but where the track turns sharp left keep forward and, ignoring a stile, walk down the left hand edge of the field towards Bardsey. Towards the bottom of the field the path bears half-right to cut the corner. Enter the wood, cross Gill Beck and walk up to enter the churchyard by a gate. The fine mediaeval church with its Saxon tower is worth a visit. Bear right round the east end of the church and leave the churchyard by another gate.

Walk straight forward along Woodacre Lane, the road signposted to East Keswick. Opposite Bardsey Village Hall and just past the Callister Parochial Hall go through a small white gate on the right and walk along the clear path with the wall of Castle Hill Nursing Home to your right and the site of the castle on the left. Pass through a gateway into a field and bear left, keeping a fence to your left, to leave the field through another gateway. Walk forward to join a cobbled drive and bear right down it. When you reach a tarmac road bear right along it, ignoring Cornmill Close and Cornmill Lane on the left. Now Bardsey Beck is on your left and you reach a crossroads. Turn left to the A58. Bus passengers will cross the main road and go left for a few yards to the bus-stop. Motorists will cross the main road, ignore Wood Lane bearing left uphill, and take the path bearing right up into the wood. Soon you join the old railway track and bear left away from the main road below you. At the next major path junction turn sharply right to return to the starting point.

ROUNDHAY PARK, SHADWELL AND SCARCROFT

WALK 5

9 miles (14¼ km); Pathfinder 683, 672; a varied ramble, mainly by field and woodland paths, through undulating pastoral countryside. Roundhay Park itself, including the Canal Gardens and Coronation House with its tropical wildlife, is worth exploring at leisure, but in view of the length of today's walk, that must probably be left for another occasion.

By bus: No. 10, 19, 21C from New Briggate to Roundhay Park (Prince's Avenue) (frequent) and walk into the old tram terminus which is now a large car park.

By car: Park at the old tram terminus (the posts which used to carry the overhead wires still survive), now a large car park, off Prince's Avenue at Roundhay Park.

From the far end of the car park follow the broad track which soon descends by a flight of steps. At the foot cross straight over the tarmac road and walk along in front of the tiers of seats, curving right towards the pavilion, but before you reach it, turn left up one of the sets of steps between the seats and cross the grass to another tarmac road coming down from the mansion up on the left. Cross it and continue forward to the brow of the hill (up to the left is the bandstand). Again cross straight over and keep forward across the grass, soon beginning to drop towards the valley and the Waterloo Lake (it was made in 1815). As you descend, bear left towards the lefthand end of the lake and walk round it on a clear path. Up to the left is a mock medieval castle gatehouse.

Having crossed a sleeper bridge, don't bear right with the main lakeside path, but fork left into the woods. Keep to the valley bottom path, which leads through the lovely Roundhay Gorge. After a time the path crosses and re-crosses the beck by a series of bridges. When the path forks, keep right on the lower path up the valley bottom, with more bridges to cross. Soon the noise of traffic on the Ring Road is prominent on the right. Shortly before you reach a tall well-built stone bridge spanning the beck, go through the gap in the wall on the right and follow the path uphill to the Ring Road.

Cross with great care and go left for a few yards to the signposted footpath opposite. This leads to Shadwell. When you reach Main Street, turn right for a few yards, then cross and go left into Holywell Lane. Where the road turns sharp left go through the gateway on the right and along the stony track signposted as a public bridleway. It passes Brandon House and various other houses before reaching a junction. Here you have a choice of routes:

The first is more pleasant but slightly less easy to follow. Go through the gateway ahead (Barn Cottage) and immediately turn right down the wallside to a stile in the bottom corner. Cross this and the track and the stile by the gate opposite and walk forward the few yards to the next stile. Now bear slightly left away from the fence on your right across the large field to a gate at the far end. Cross the stile by the gate and keep forward on the same line up the slope of the next field. Soon you will see that you are making for a large white gate. When you reach it, don't go through, but head back across the field at an angle of 90 degrees to the path you have just been following to a stile which is visible as a fenced gap in the far hedge between two large trees. There is no clear path through these fields. Cross the stile and bear slightly left to walk at right angles to the hedge you have just crossed over the next field. As

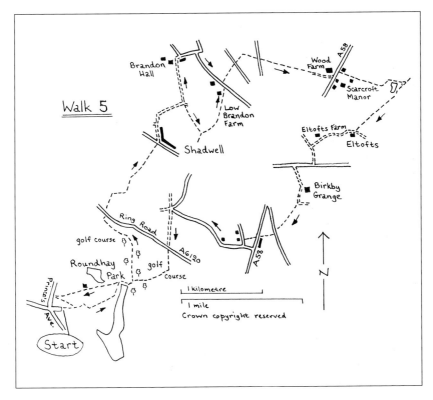

you come over the crest you will see that you are heading for a gate in the next facing hedge. Pass through and bear half right to a stile in the next hedge, cross and turn left and follow the hedge down to a footbridge in the field corner. Cross and bear half left to a stile onto a minor road. Turn left for about 75 yards and keep a lookout for a signpost and stile on the right.

The second alternative is easy to follow, but can be excessively muddy due to heavy usage by horses and involves more road-walking. Fork left down a narrower fenced path and follow it to the T-junction at Brandon Hall Farm, where you bear right to reach a minor road. Keep straight forward along this and turn sharp right at the next junction. At the end of a stretch of wall on the left with a hedge growing on top of it you will reach a signposted footpath on the left.

The path leads through a young plantation, keeping close to the hedge/fence on the left, and over a stile into a fenced path past a nursery to another stile and the next motor road. Cross straight over to the stile opposite, just to the left of the entrance to White Hall. Follow the fence/hedge on your right, and where it bears right keep with it (it is now a fence/wall) to a stile in the corner. The path leads to a track which you follow down to the next road. Again cross straight over to another stile, then follow the wall/fence/hedge on your left. Pass through the gateway in the far corner (or cross the stile) and continue forward across the next field. A hedge comes down from the left and again you have a fence/hedge to your left. Pass through two more gateways and follow the track to the A58 Leeds to Wetherby road at Wood Farm.

Cross with care and turn left along the pavement for 60 yards to a footpath on the right signposted to Thorner. Walk up the drive towards Scarcroft Manor, but leave it just before the next gateway and pass to the left of the lodge along a narrow path initially between high walls. Cross a stile into parkland and follow the hedge/fence on your left down until shortly after reaching a wood on the left you come to a stile into it. Walk along the track to a junction with a gate ahead and the track bearing left through an old gateway, and cross the stile on the right to continue down a track through the wood. Cross the bridge by the sluice at the lefthand end of the lake and in a few yards fork right on a track which rises to the top edge of the wood. The lake is down to your right.

The clear path keeps forward some way above the lake, then continues through the wood until it leaves this through a kissing-gate. Keep straight forward across the next field, heading for a cluster of houses in the distance. Leave the field by a stile just below the houses

(Eltofts) and bear right along the lane, soon joining the access drive to Eltofts House (which is behind you). Shortly after passing Eltofts Farm the road turns left. At the motor road turn right, then after 250 yards turn left into the access road to Birkby. As the road bears left towards the buildings fork right off it and follow the hedge on the right into a broad fenced track. The track leads through a gateway into a field and turns left. Leave it here and bear slightly right over the field to a stile in the next hedge just to the left of a power line pole.

Bear diagonally left across the next large field to a yellow marker post in the far hedge. When you reach it, keep forward with the hedge to your left to the road. Cross it and go left for a short distance to a signposted footpath opposite. Follow the hedge on the left to the next road, the A58 again. Cross to the stile opposite and walk straight over the next field to a stile by a gate just to the left of a large house. Turn left along the road, then go right at the T-junction.

When you reach the 30 m.p.h. limit on the edge of Shadwell the road makes a sharp turn right. On this bend you must ignore the track ahead, turn left, then immediately fork left again on a track across the field. It leads once more to the Leeds Ring Road. Cross with care to the stile opposite. Walk straight forward over the golf course, heeding the notice to beware of flying balls. You reach some trees, and immediately after crossing a tiny beck fork right off the track down a couple of steps onto a clear path across more of the golf course towards the woods. Cross straight over a clear cross path and enter the wood, at first with an old wall to your left. Pass through a gap in a facing wall, cross another cross path and continue downhill through woodland. On the way you go up and then down a few steps.

Rejoin your outward route and bear left to the lake, there turning right over the sleeper bridge. Having rounded the end of the lake bear right up the slope with a wood to your right and you will reach the upper lake. Bear left to the bandstand we saw earlier, cross straight over the road and take the tarmac drive opposite, passing to the left of the mansion, built in 1826 and called by Pevsner 'the grandest of the Late Georgian mansions of Leeds'. This broad drive leads to the main gates of the Park and the bus stop. For the car park bear left shortly before reaching the Park gates.

BARWICK IN ELMET AND SAW WOOD

WALK 6

5 miles (8 km); Pathfinder Map 683. Arable, pastoral and woodland.

By bus: No. 56/57 Tinshill/Ireland Wood-Leeds (St. John's Centre, Headrow, Eastgate) -Barwick, half-hourly, Sundays hourly; 64/64A Leeds (Infirmary Street, Boar Lane, Call Lane) -Barwick-Aberford, half-hourly, hourly evenings and Sundays.
By car: There is limited parking in Barwick Main Street, or park in Elmwood Lane, which is parallel to Main Street but west of it.

The walk starts at the maypole in the centre of Barwick in Elmet. From the maypole walk past the side of the Gascoigne Arms along a street called The Boyle. Almost at once there is a junction: leave The Boyle, which forks right, and keep straight on along Elmwood Lane, which soon bends left. Turn right into Elmwood Avenue; between houses 30 and 32 on the right take the tarmac ginnel which soon turns right, and when the garden wall ends keep straight forward down the left hand edge of the field. After 40 yards cross a stile in the hedge on the left and continue down the next field, bearing left away from the hedge, to a gap in the hedge at the bottom. Turn left along the tarmac road.

After the tarmac ends at Rakehill Farm keep forward along the track for about 300 yards, then follow the footpath sign pointing right into a field. Walk along the edge of the field with a hedge to your left. Cross the stile in the top corner and turn sharp left. Where the hedge on your left turns sharp left again the footpath turns right across the middle of the field. After 50 yards at a marker post turn left again to the next marker post, where again you turn sharp right and now head towards the right hand edge of the wood in the distance. The houses of Scholes are off to your left. At the next post turn left again, and in 50 yards at the next one turn right again. Pass the end of a hedge, and now you have the remains of a hedge and a ditch on your left. The track passes to the right of the wood.

Follow the track to Woodhouse Farm and there turn left along the farm access track. At a fork just before Whinmoor Nook Farm bear right to the A64 Leeds to York road. Cross straight over this busy road into the field opposite and walk forward along its left hand edge. Follow the high wire fence when it turns left, and at the next field corner turn right, with the track of the old Leeds to Wetherby railway line to your left. In a few yards ignore a stone bridge over the railway and keep forward along the lefthand edge of the field. About 80 yards before a tall metal pylon take a broad track left which crosses the railway line, but turn right off it along the old bed of the railway. After a time pass through a metal kissing-gate.

About 100 yards before a double gate across the railway track with a tree to the left of it and a kissing-gate to the left of the tree, go through a kissing-gate by a gate on the right and walk straight over the field, passing a wooden pylon, soon with a hedge to your left. The houses of Thorner are off to your left. When the hedge on the left ends keep forward on the path, which leads to the left of another hedge ahead. Follow this hedge to the far corner of the field and turn right through a kissing-gate into a broad hedged way.

Walk along the hedged lane to the corner of the wood. Immediately after entering the wood fork half-left (yellow waymark) on a clear path through the wood. Follow this clear path forward through Saw Wood, ignoring cross paths, and reassured from time to time by marker posts with yellow arrows. You reach the A64 again opposite Flying Horse Farm. Turn right along the road for about 50 yards then cross it with great care to a signposted path opposite. Cross the stile and walk forward with the hedge/fence to your left. When this turns left keep forward along the old field boundary soon once more with a hedge to your left.

Cross the stile at the bottom and follow the very clear path forward across the next field. Woodhouse Farm is up to your right. At a signposted path junction bear left, soon passing through a gap in the hedge ahead and following the hedge on your right. When the hedge ends keep forward with a ditch to your right. At a metal pylon fork half-right across the ditch to a signpost, then forward across the middle of the field to a tree 40 yards ahead, then follow the same line to a marker post. At this point, an old field corner, turn sharp left and follow the field boundary with a hedge to your right. Keep with the field edge when it turns right, cross the stile in the next field corner and keep on with the hedge to your right to another stile ahead, by a gate on the right. Now the hedge is on your left. Cross another stile and a footbridge and walk forward for a few yards before bearing slightly left to a signpost in the top lefthand corner of the field. Turn left along the road and at the next junction bear right with it uphill back into Barwick.

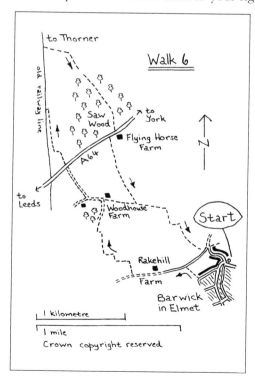

25

BARWICK IN ELMET AND
GARFORTH CIRCULAR VIA BARNBOW LANE

WALK 7

6½ miles (10 km). Pathfinder 683. Gently undulating countryside east of Leeds, including part of the Leeds Country Way.

By bus: No. 56/57 Tinshill/Ireland Wood-Leeds (St. John's Centre, Headrow, Eastgate) -Barwick, half-hourly, Sundays hourly; 64/64A Leeds (Infirmary Street, Boar Lane, Call Lane) -Barwick-Aberford, half-hourly, hourly evenings and Sundays.

By car: There is limited parking in Barwick Main Street, or park in Elmwood Lane, which is parallel to Main Street but west of it.

The walk starts at the maypole in the centre of Barwick in Elmet. From the maypole walk past the side of the Gascoigne Arms along a street called The Boyle. Almost at once there is a junction: leave The Boyle, which forks right, and keep straight on along Elmwood Lane, which soon bends left. At a crossroads turn right into Carrfield Road. Ignore the garage access lane on the left and after 100 yards turn left into the first street, (Carrfield Road 44-64) which soon ends at a turning space, but straight ahead there is a fenced ginnel, which leads to a main road. Turn left for a few yards, then right into Flats Lane. Between numbers 32 and 34 turn right into a fenced ginnel leading to a stile. Bear half left across the narrowish field to the next stile.

Now some care is needed with route finding, although the path should be visible on the ground. From the stile walk straight forward for a few yards to cross a beck. Looking half left over the field you will see a fence: you are making for a stile near the left hand end of this fence. So bear half left towards the line of an old hedge, then follow it to the stile. Cross this and walk straight forward to the left hand end of the hedge ahead. Bear right up the slope with the hedge to your left. Follow the edge of this field to the top corner, then turn left through the hedge, and continue with the hedge now on your right.

Crossing the rise, Garforth can be seen ahead. Follow the hedge down, crossing two stiles, to reach a third stile into a wood (FP sign pointing left to Barwick Road and Parlington, back to Barwick and right to Manor Farm and Garforth). Follow the right hand path, which leads between Garforth golf course on the left and a tall hedge on the right. Route finding on the next stretch, until you leave the golf course again, is made easier by tall wooden marker posts with yellow tops, which indicate the right of way. As you cross several fairways, there is some danger from flying golf balls. The path bears left through the wood to the edge of the golf course, then straight forward to cross a footbridge.

Keep straight on up the slight slope with a hedge to your left, and just before the field corner a marker post points you through the hedge on the left. Bear slightly left over the fairway to the next marker post on the edge of a wood, and walk through the wood to the next post on the far side, then keep forward across the next fairway to a cluster of low trees with a white marker post on the nearside edge. Now bear slightly left through the trees to the next tall post, crossing a gravel path on the way, and at this post bear left along a track, which is a bridleway between Barnbow Lane and Garforth, passing a row of young conifers on your right, to the next post, which is just before the track enters trees.

Turn right and walk to the next post on the far side of a wide sleeper bridge. Now turn left and follow Cock Beck on your left through trees to the next post. Turn right and follow the boundary fence/hedge of the golf course up to a large old footpath sign. Ignore the stile on the left and turn right along the top edge of the wood. Pass along the lefthand

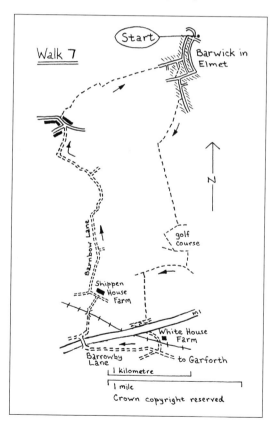

edge of the 4th tee and at the far side bear left to follow a hedge on your left along through trees. In about 25 yards bear left along a broad path, soon forking left up to the 6th tee. Again keep along the lefthand edge. As you walk on along the top edge of the golf course look out for a marker post on the left which points you along a path between the hedge on the left and a narrow strip of trees on the right.

Follow the hedge until you leave the woodland (and the golf course, there is a warning notice-board), and walk on along the edge of the field, keeping the hedge on your left. In 50 yards the hedge ends: here turn left and head for a wooden pylon bearing power lines. About 50 yards before you reach it cross a stile ahead and continue forward with the fence to your left to a stile in the next field corner. Cross this and follow the fence/hedge on your left over three more stiles to reach a track with the motorway embankment straight ahead. Turn right along the track for 60 yards, then go left through the underpass under the motorway. Bear half left up the track, soon passing through a gate. Follow the track to White House Farm, enter the yard and bear right to cross the main Leeds-York railway (CARE!). Follow the lane to its end.

Here you join the Leeds Country Way. Turn right, taking the right hand of the two lanes which present themselves (Barrowby Lane) (Garforth is along the road to the left), and follow it until it swings right over a motorway bridge. On the far side bear right and then left and follow the track down to cross the railway again and reach Shippen House Farm. Turn left along the lane, and at the next fork keep right. Soon the metalled road becomes a track (Barnbow Lane). Keep on the main track, ignoring tracks to right or left; a field's breadth before the houses at Scholes it curves sharply right; follow it to the main road. Cross this, go right the few yards to the junction, then bear left; cross this road too, and just before the road bends left, before a bus stop, turn right into a track (Leeds Country Way sign).

The track follows the hedge on the left. Where the track ends, go through a very wide gap in the hedge on the left and continue the direction as before, now on a footpath with the hedge to your right. Soon you pass under power lines. In the corner of the field cross a stile on the right and the hedge is now to your left. After 50 yards find a stile on the left, cross it and continue with the hedge to your left. In the field corner cross through a gap on the left to continue your direction now with the hedge to your right. After a time you join a hedged lane, then a macadamed street which leads back to your outward route. At the crossroads either turn left to return to the maypole or keep straight on for Main Street.

BARWICK IN ELMET TO PARLINGTON PARK

WALK 8

8 miles (13 km); Pathfinder 683, 684. Pleasantly undulating countryside, arable, pasture and woodland; good paths.

By bus: No. 56/57 Tinshill/Ireland Wood-Leeds (St. John's Centre, Headrow, Eastgate) -Barwick, half-hourly, Sundays hourly; 64/64A Leeds (Infirmary Street, Boar Lane, Call Lane) -Barwick-Aberford, half-hourly, hourly evenings and Sundays.

By car: There is limited parking in Barwick Main Street, or park in Elmwood Lane, which is parallel to Main Street but west of it.

The walk starts at the maypole in the centre of Barwick in Elmet. From the maypole walk past the side of the Gascoigne Arms along a street called The Boyle. Almost at once there is a junction: fork right and continue along The Boyle, following it through the village and downhill. Where it forks (the left hand branch is Rakehill Road) keep right (footpath sign) and after the tarmac ends cross Rake Beck by the footbridge and continue along the track. You are on the Leeds Country Way. At the end of the track keep forward through the gap in the hedge by the footpath sign and keep forward with a hedge to your left. Shortly after the hedge ends there is a redundant stile; keep forward and cross Potterton Beck by a footbridge.

Cross the stile on the left and walk parallel to the beck on your left. Follow the beck, crossing several stiles, all the way to a stile just before the A64 Leeds to York road. Here you leave the Leeds Country Way. Don't cross this stile, but turn right with the fence/wall to your left until you reach another stile in it. Don't cross this one either, but head back across the field, aiming just to the right of the small wood, and keeping the trees on your left follow them along to a redundant stile; at this point bear slightly left and keep the remainder of the trees to your right, shortly with a fence on your left, to reach a stile. Cross and look right to find the next stile, cross it and walk forward to the next stile, then continue with a fence and soon a hedge on your right. Cross another stile and turn right, still with the hedge to your right. In the next corner turn left again and follow the hedge to a road.

Bear right along it, ignoring the access road to the farm on the right, and at the next junction ignore Potterton Lane on the right and keep straight on. Where the road turns sharp left, with the entrance into Potterton Hall ahead, turn right along a track (Miry Lane). Follow this all the way to where it drops into a dip and reaches a T-junction. Turn

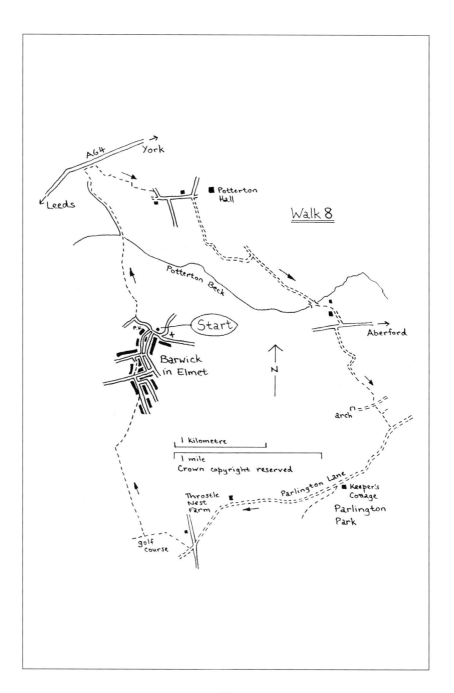

A64   York

Leeds

■ Potterton Hall

Walk 8

Potterton Beck

Start

P.O. ✚

Barwick in Elmet

N

Aberford

arch

1 kilometre

1 mile
Crown copyright reserved

Parlington Lane

Throstle Nest Farm

■ Keeper's Cottage

Parlington Park

golf course

right, with a deep ditch on the right. Shortly after bending slightly left the track passes through an embankment called on the map The Ridge, and at the foot of the next field it turns left. Just before a pond turn right off the main track and follow the path until you cross Cock Beck and reach a gate into a field. Bear half-left over the next field to pass through a line of trees onto a track which climbs the bank, passing well to the right of an isolated house, and just to the left of the farm buildings, to a gate in the top corner. Leaving Leyfield Farm to your right, follow the track to the Barwick to Aberford road.

Turn right for a few yards, then cross and go through the large double gate into a narrow wood. You have now entered the Parlington Estate. The route through the wood is marked by large yellow arrows painted on trees. The wood widens and the track curves left: keep left at the fork on this bend. When you reach the edge of the wood at a field corner, the track turns sharply right and climbs gently to the other edge of the wood. Here bear left and follow the path up to the right of the wood, but at the top edge of the field on your right keep straight forward through the trees to reach another large field. On the far side you will see a stile by a gate, and there should be a clear path across to it. The houses of Aberford can now be seen to your left.

From the stile bear slightly right to cross a tarmac road (look right to see the triumphal arch, erected in 1783 to commemorate 'Liberty in N.America triumphant') and descend right to a fence corner, where you bear left with the fence to your right. Follow the fence to the next stile and turn right along the track (Parlington Lane). When you reach a fork keep right on the main track to pass through a tunnel. Pass to the right of Keeper's Cottage, ignoring the entrance gates on the right. At the next houses, the Old Coal Staith, ignore a track forking left. Ignore an access road on the right to Throstle Nest Farm, cross Cock Beck and follow the track, now with a tarmac surface, to the Barwick to Garforth road.

Immediately opposite is the access road to Willow Park Farm: follow this for 60 yards to a footpath sign pointing right through the hedge onto Garforth Golf Club's course. The right of way across the golf course is marked by tall wooden marker posts with yellow tops. So walk straight across the fairways to the next post, taking care not to be struck by flying golf balls. The post after that is just before a small wood, and to find the next one you have to continue your line through the trees. From it you can see the next post by the hedge on the far side. Bear left there, keeping the hedge to your right, passing the 18th tee and entering woodland. When you reach a large wooden signpost and a stile on the right cross this and follow the hedge/fence on your left up through several fields, Barwick appearing half-right ahead as you cross the rise.

Where the remains of the hedge begin to bear right cross through it (marker post) and turn right, now with the hedge to your right. The path descends gently and bears left to a stile. Cross this, pass to the left of a blackthorn bush, and you will see the next stile in the facing hedge. Cross and bear half-left over the next field to a stile leading into a ginnel. At the street turn left, and at the main road there is a bus stop for buses back to Leeds. To return to the maypole cross the main road and go left, for a couple of yards to find a ginnel on the right. Follow this to its end, walk forward along the street to the T-junction, turn right and at the next main road go left to return to the village centre.

KIPPAX TO MICKLEFIELD AND LEDSHAM

WALK 9

9 miles (14¼ km); Pathfinder 684. An easy ramble in the limestone belt east of Leeds, woodland, pasture and parkland. The only drawback is one nasty crossing of the A1: I recommend doing this walk at the weekend, when the road can be quieter. (When the A1 is upgraded to motorway status, a safe crossing will be provided at this point.)

By bus: No. 163, 164, 165, 166 Castleford bus from outside the Bond Street Centre in Boar Lane, Leeds to the centre of Kippax (every 10 minutes, half-hourly evenings and Sundays).
By car: there is a car park about 50 yards below the west tower of Kippax Parish Church on the south side.

Walk up and enter the churchyard by the west tower of the fine Norman church. Turn left before the tower and keep close to the lefthand edge of the churchyard. The path soon bears right and leaves the churchyard through a gate on the east side. Turn left along the tarmac ginnel, then right at the T-junction, still with part of the churchyard to your right. Keep forward to a road junction and continue straight on along Sandgate Terrace. Where the allotments on the left end go left along a track, and where the track curves left into the allotments and the path ahead forks, ignore the tarmac path forking right (our return route) and keep straight on.

About 70 yards after leaving the last houses of Kippax the path forks: keep right, passing to the left of a wooden pylon. After a time the track swings left, becomes metalled and reaches a cross track. Turn right and follow this track to the A63. Turn right, soon crossing the road to the footway on the other side. At the roundabout cross straight over the A656 and continue along the A63 for another 400 yards until you turn left at a bridleway sign along a track. Cross straight over a tarmac road, and continue along the track. Ignore a track forking left to Warren Farm and follow the line of overhead power lines forward. Pass round the end of a wooden fence, and now you have a wire fence on the right.

On reaching houses the path broadens to a track again and then becomes a tarmac road. At the roundabout ignore the road on the right and walk straight forward to cross the Leeds to York railway line (care!). Follow the track forward, with a football ground to the right and the houses of Micklefield over to the left. Beyond the football pitch there is a children's playground to the right of the track. Just before the track reaches a motor road fork left along a tarmac footpath which crosses a small concrete bridge and rises to Micklefield. Immediately after the school turn right and walk forward to reach the village street, the Old Great North Road, with the Blands Arms (Samuel Smith) a few yards to the right.

Cross the road and take the signposted track opposite. At the A1 the track bears left, and at the top of the slope you turn right to cross the bridge over the A1. On the far side turn right again. At the next junction keep forward, still with the A1 to your right. About 20 yards before the track crosses a beck, with filter beds beyond, fork left off it along another track, parallel to the beck over on your right and heading towards woodland. The track enters the woods. Follow it until 15 yards before it leaves the top side of the wood through a gate you fork right along a clear path. Eventually it bears slightly right and drops to emerge from the wood with a high railway embankment to the left. Follow this forward until you turn left and pass through a tunnel under the railway.

Bear half left with the track across the field to the next wood. A few yards after you reach the trees turn right off the track (marker post) along a clear but narrow path. Soon you must cross the railway line to Selby (care again!). Soon there is a steep drop to the right of the path and you must bear right round the edge of this, ignoring a path forking left on this bend. A short distance further on you reach another fork, where you take the left branch ahead. When you reach a clear cross track turn right along it. A few yards before you reach the A1 again fork right up to it.

It is dual carriageway, so you can take it in two parts, climbing the crash barrier between them, but visibility is not very good to the right and

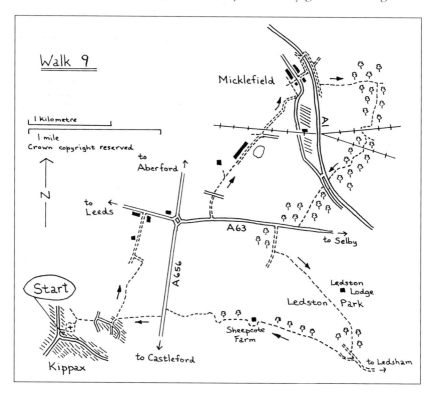

Walk 9

1 Kilometre

1 mile
Crown copyright reserved

N

Micklefield

to
Aberford

to
Leeds

A63

to Selby

Start

A656

Ledston
Lodge
Ledston   Park

Sheepcote
Farm

to Castleford

to Ledsham

Kippax

the road is usually very busy. Having safely reached the other side, cross another minor road and go left for a few yards to enter the wood through a gateway just to the right of a bench. The path stays fairly close to the righthand edge of the wood. When you reach a fork, keep left, and a few yards further on left again, and you will emerge on to the A63 again. Turn right along it, as far as the start of the next wood on the lefthand side of the road; here cross the road and follow the sign pointing left along a track with the wood on your right. Where this wood ends, another sign points left over a stile. Walk along the clear grassy path through recently planted trees, with a young wood to the right.

The next stile leads into Ledston Park, an enormous expanse of parkland, where the going is attractive but navigation none too easy. There are waymark posts to guide you through, but these have a tendency to be knocked over by livestock. From the stile bear slightly right up the grass, aiming for what looks in the distance like a gap between the woodland on the left and that on the right. You should soon pick up a clear narrow trod. As you breast the first rise you will see a group of three mature trees close together: the path passes between them, then bears slightly left to pass through the various groups of trees. Look left to see the well-preserved 17th-century Ledston Lodge.

Soon you must bear slightly right, still down through the park, almost parallel to, but gradually approaching the wood on the left. As you come over the rise you will see that you are heading for a stile into the woods. Cross the stile and walk along the track. When you reach an access road, bear left down it. At the next junction, going left would take you into the lovely village of Ledsham, with its Saxon church and refreshments in the Chequers Inn, but the walk turns sharp right (public footpath sign) along another track.

Where the track forks, keep following the edge of the wood on your right. Where this ends, keep straight forward with a field boundary to your right. Cross a stile in a piece of fence ahead, and once more you have a wood to your right. Soon a stile by a gate ahead takes you into a field, and now you are separated from the wood by a gallop. Keep along with the fence on your right, cross a stile in the next corner, and continue by the fence until you reach a stile in it. Cross this, then the gallop, then the next stile and in a few yards another stile, and walk forward with the wall of Sheepcote Farm to your right. Where this turns sharp right, bear very slightly right over the field (the farmhouse is to your right) to a stile in a fence corner, and continue with a fence and soon yet another wood to your right.

Cross a wooden footbridge and turn right, still following the edge of the wood. Pass through a gap in a facing hedge and continue along the right hand edge of the field with a narrow strip of woodland to the right. Follow the field edge to the A656 and turn left along the footway. In about 80 yards cross the road and take the signposted tarmac path back to Kippax. At the allotments you rejoin your outward route, which you re-trace back to your starting-point.

KIPPAX TO LEDSHAM, FAIRBURN INGS AND LEDSTON

WALK 10

7½ miles (12 km); Pathfinder 684, 693. An easy walk along clear paths and tracks, through gently undulating countryside, with the possibility of a visit to a well-known RSPB reserve.

By bus: No. 163, 164, 165, 166 Castleford bus from outside the Bond Street Centre in Boar Lane, Leeds to the centre of Kippax (every 10 minutes, half-hourly evenings and Sundays).
By car: there is a car park about 50 yards below the west tower of Kippax Parish Church on the south side.

Walk up and enter the churchyard by the west tower of the fine Norman church. Turn left before the tower and keep close to the lefthand edge of the churchyard. The path soon bears right and leaves the churchyard through a gate on the east side. Turn left along the tarmac ginnel, then right at the T-junction, still with part of the churchyard to your right. Keep forward to a road junction and continue straight on along Sandgate Terrace. Where the allotments on the left end go left along a track, and at the next path junction keep right on the tarmac path across the fields.

When you reach the A656 Castleford to Aberford road (a very straight Roman road) cross to the footway and turn left for 100 yards to a tarmac

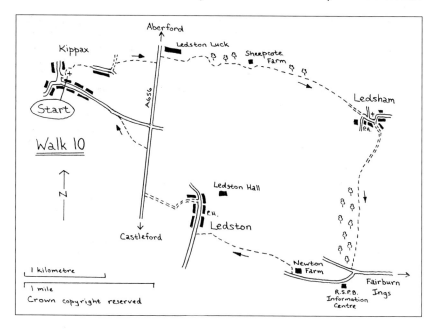

path on the right down into the field, near the former Ledston Luck colliery. The path follows the left hand edge of the field. When you reach the end of a wood on the left, the path turns sharp left over a wooden footbridge, then continues along the field edge. At Sheepcote Farm follow the fence on your left, and when it ends keep forward across the field to a wall corner, and follow the wall on your left up to another stile (redundant), then forward to another stile and over the gritted gallop to another stile. Bear left round the edge of the field.

Cross the stile in the far corner of the field and continue with the fence and gallop to your left to the next stile, where the path joins the gallop. At the end of the wood cross the stile in the fence ahead and keep forward along the left hand edge of the field (do not be tempted to cross left into the next field). Soon you have another wood to the left and after a time the path becomes a clear track which enters woodland. You are joined by another track from the left and in a short distance you reach Ledsham. Walk straight through this lovely village, keeping the Chequers Inn on your right and the most interesting Saxon parish church on the left.

Immediately after the church, where the road bears left, turn right along a No Through Road. After 150 yards fork left onto a narrower tarmac lane which soon becomes an unsurfaced track. The track narrows to a path, and Ferrybridge Power Station is prominent ahead. The path soon reaches a wood and keeps along its left hand edge, which it follows to the next road. The large lake which appears half-left ahead is Fairburn Ings Nature Reserve.

Turn left along the road, then right at the T-junction. Just after passing a large RSPB car park on the left there is the entrance to the Fairburn Ings Information Centre, where there is also a hide. Follow the motor road past Newton Farm on the right. Just beyond it the road bends right then left: leave it on this bend to turn up an access road on the right. In a few yards fork right into a field and follow the fence on the left along to another stile. Cross this and walk up the slope. At the top turn left along a clear cross track. The view left is over Newton Ings to Castleford.

Soon the track passes under power lines carried by wooden pylons then follows them along. When it passes under them again and they bear slightly left over the field and the track bears right, keep forward along the old field boundary. Shortly after you pick up a hedge on the left, a signpost points you half-right across the field – there should be a clear path. Cross the stile on the far side and walk down the edge of the next field with the fence to your right. Cross the stile and turn right along the road through Ledston, another attractive village.

Near the far end of Ledston turn left along Green Lane (there is a view half-right up to Ledston Hall). At Ledston School the surface ends and the track leads back to the A656. Cross to the footway and turn right along the road for 500 yards to where a footpath signpost points left through the hedge. Follow the clear path over the fields to the next road, and turn left along it to return to Kippax.

LOTHERTON HALL FROM GARFORTH OR ABERFORD

WALK 11

9 miles (14½ km) or 5 miles (8 km); Pathfinder 684. The Edwardian Lotherton Hall was given to Leeds by the Gascoigne family in 1968 and is now one of the Leeds art museums, specialising in oriental pottery and porcelain and in costume. The Bird Garden is popular with children. The House is closed on Mondays.

By train: (longer walk) Leeds to East Garforth Station (York & Selby Line).
By bus: (shorter walk) No. 64/64A from Leeds Infirmary Street to Aberford (half-hourly, hourly evenings and Sundays) (walk south along the main street until you reach Lotherton Lane, turn left along it and join the walk description at [*] below).
By car: the most convenient starting point is Lotherton Hall (GR 449 360) (join the walk description at [#] below).

The start of the walk is dull, but after a few minutes we are out in the country. Having left the train from Leeds, don't cross the tall red footbridge, but walk past it down the slope and where the tarmac path forks keep left. Follow the path up to where it ends at a cross street, turn left for a few yards then right along Harlech Way. Turn along the first street on the left, Stirling Way, then go left at the next T-junction for a few yards to find a fenced ginnel on the right with allotments to the right of it. When you reach a tarmac path turn right along it, soon entering another unsurfaced ginnel ahead which leads to a main road (the A642). Cross over and turn right, but in a short distance turn left down Ash Lane. Where it forks keep right, then straight along the track to the right of the factory yard and so on to the old Fly Line (former railway).

Pass under the M1, then just before a brick house on the right, ignore a right and then a left fork, and when you reach a cross track, keep forward through a squeeze stile and along a narrower path. On your way through the wood ignore a clear path forking left. Cross straight over a cross track and follow the path to another squeeze stile, where you join Parlington Lane. Keep forward past the Gamekeeper's Cottage, ignoring a track bearing left through a gate, and follow the track through the longer and the shorter tunnel all the way to Aberford. Cross straight over the old A1 and along Lotherton Lane. [*] The road bears right and then left under the A1. Take the first road on the left. On a right hand bend ignore another road forking left.

Follow the road to where it is crossed by a band of trees and a low mound: this is The Rein, believed to be an Iron Age boundary. Turn right off the road a few yards beyond this through a large gateway and follow the track with the trees to the right to the next motor road. Turn right along this, then left along the next minor road (signposted Sherburn in Elmet), and when this bends left, fork right off it into the grounds of Lotherton Hall, passing a large car park on the left.

When you reach the buildings, either bear right to return to the car, or keep forward to [#] pass between the stable block and the Hall and continue along a paved path to pass through some trees and a gate into a paddock. Walk straight through, and leave it by a kissing-gate in the far right hand corner. A clear path leads forward through the fields.

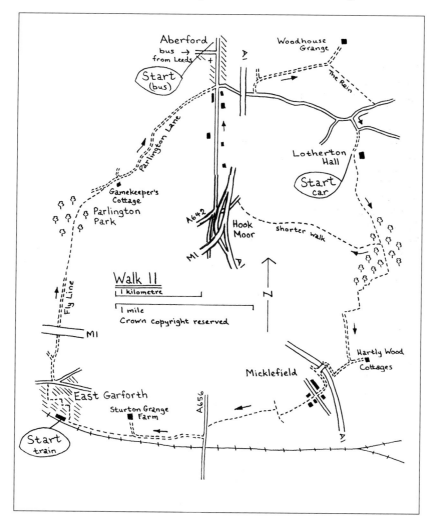

39

Shortly after picking up woodland on the left, the path itself enters the woods through a gate.

Pass a large gate which doesn't seem to have a purpose, and keep on between bushes. When you reach a clear cross track, the SHORT WALK turns right and follows the track through Bragdale all the way to the road near Hook Moor, traffic on the A1 becoming increasingly noticeable as you walk. Turn left along the road to pass under the M1 and then the A1, then take the first road on the right (signposted Aberford), pass one of the entrances to Parlington Park on the left and follow this Roman road, the old A1, back to Aberford (there is a footway on the left), noticing the Victorian Gothic Gascoigne Almshouses on the left on the way.

The LONG WALK crosses straight over the cross track (signpost to Micklefield) along a clear woodland path. When you reach a fork keep left, i.e. straight on. At the far end of the wood you join a track. Ignore the track to the left, walk forward for a few yards and at the fork take the right hand track along the outside edge of the wood. Follow this track until the wood on the right ends, then ignore the track straight ahead and turn sharp left on another track through the fields. Just over the rise, with Hartly Wood Cottages up to the left, you meet a cross track: turn right down it towards Micklefield. Just before the A1 turn right at another T-junction and follow this track when it turns left to cross the A1 by a bridge. On the far side turn left again, and the track soon bears right to Micklefield.

Cross straight over the main street, passing to the left of the fish shop, then to the right of the school, and forward on a grassy track through the fields. When you meet a cross track turn right for 20 yards, then left off it onto a narrow path along an old field boundary. Eventually you find yourself walking to the left of an old barbed-wire fence which leads to a stile in the next field corner. Cross this and continue forward across the middle of the next field to the Roman Road (A656).

Cross the road and turn left. About 50 yards after the access road to Sturton Grange Farm on the right turn right at the footpath sign with a fence on your left. Soon you are walking on the grass parallel to the access road. When this bears right to the farm and another track goes left over a railway bridge, keep forward over the stile by the gate and walk along the field edge with a fence to the left. Cross another three stiles and continue forward along the road. When the road bears right. keep forward along the tarmac path to return to East Garforth Station. Motorists should fork right along a tarmac path just before reaching the footbridge over the railway and then go back to the start of the walk description.

BRAMHAM PARK AND HAZLEWOOD CASTLE

WALK 12

11¼ miles (18 km); Pathfinder 673, 684; an easy ramble, mainly on good tracks and field paths, through the pastoral and wooded countryside of the Magnesian limestone belt east of Leeds.

By bus: No. 770 Wetherby bus from Leeds Central Bus Station to Bramham (half-hourly, evenings and Sundays hourly).
By car: Park on the old Great North Road in Bramham – there is a suitable layby just south of the village (GR 424 425).

Make your way to the main crossroads in the village centre. Have a stroll through this lovely limestone village, up to the Norman church, before returning to this point. Face the war memorial, with the Red Lion on your left, then walk half-right to take the No Through Road to the left of Bay House called Almshouse Hill. Follow it steeply up, bearing left to pass through the bollards, ignore Crag Gardens forking left, join Freely Lane and bear left along it. The large house over the high wall at the top of the slope is Bramham Lodge.

When you reach the main road cross straight over into the No Through Road opposite. After the tarmac ends keep forward along the unsurfaced track to meet another narrow motor road. Again cross straight over and walk along the drive to Headley Hall. When the drive forks bear right, passing to the right of a long low building, towards a prominent water tower. Here fork left again, still on the surfaced track. Immediately before you reach a large building set back on the right, turn right off the track and pass first to the right of this building, then bear left along behind it past the silos. At the far end turn right along a track into a field, then left along the left hand edge of this field, following a row of power lines. Pass through a gateway at the end of the field and turn sharp right along the edge of the next field, now with the fence to your right. The noisy A64 is now ahead of you. At the end of the field bear left with the field boundary, to reach the main road over a stile.

Turn right along the footway until you reach a large layby, then cross the A64 with great care, using gaps in the crash barrier, into a minor road opposite. When this turns right to Hazlewood Castle Hotel, keep straight on along the farm road. At Beck House Farm the track bears right and leads to Hazlewood Castle. With the old entrance to the castle immediately ahead (it's worth taking a look inside the courtyard at the late 13th-century chapel and the Georgian rebuilding of the castle) turn sharp left and in a few yards ignore a track forking right. Turn into the next track on the right by a small barn, but only for about 50 yards, until

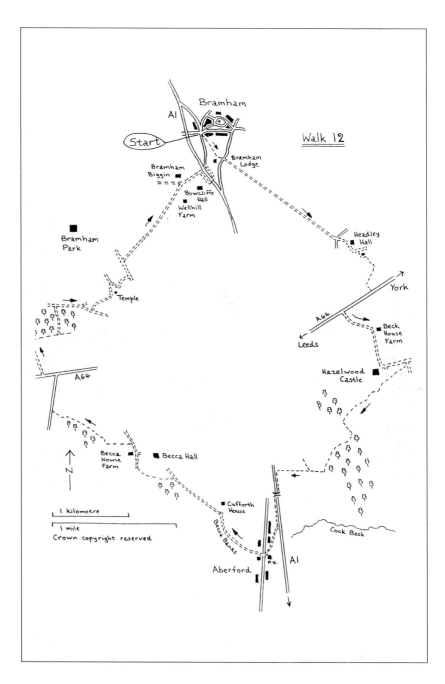

Bramham

A1

Start

Walk 12

Bramham
Lodge

Bramham
Biggin

Bowcliffe
Hall
Wellhill
Farm

Bramham
Park

Headley
Hall

Temple

York

A64

Leeds

Beck
House
Farm

Hazelwood
Castle

A64

Becca
Home
Farm

Becca Hall

N

Cufforth
House

Cock Beck

1 kilometre

1 mile
Crown copyright reserved

Becca Banks

P.H.

A1

Aberford

you reach a stile on the right. Walk up the right hand edge of the field, passing a filter-bed and a small copse. Cross another stile and bear right, then left, round the field edge. There is a fine view of the castle to your right.

Follow the field edge over a stile by a gate and on to another stile into a small wood. Walk forward through this, passing the end of a wall and on with a fence to your right. At the far end of the wood turn left along a track, but only for about 35 yards until a marker post points half-right towards the right hand of the two small woods you will see ahead. Pass diagonally through this wood, keeping fairly close to its right hand side, emerge from the wood at a marker post, turn left along the edge of the wood for a few yards, then walk half right across the field to a gap in a fence (crossing a gallop on the way) and then to an old hedge where there is a footpath sign. Turn left along the track towards a large wood. When you reach this, leave the track and turn right along its outside edge.

When you reach a point where the wood goes sharp left and a signpost points both right and back the way you have come, turn right along the track, but where this curves right, keep straight forward across the large field, passing under the power lines. Cross the stile and turn left along the fenced path, with the A1 down on your right. Cross it by the footbridge and turn left down another fenced path. At the bottom of the slope pass through the gate and turn right and follow the track and then the road into Aberford, reaching the main road by a small triangular green and the Arabian Horse pub.

Cross the main road to the tarmac lane between houses opposite (Becca Lane), which is an old access drive to Becca Hall. The Iron Age embankment of Becca Banks is to the left of the drive. Ignore the drive forking right to Cufforth House and when the tarmac ends keep forward along the unsurfaced track to pass a lodge. After some distance the wood on the left comes back to join the track, and at the end of this wood fork half-left off the track (waymark). Keep the wood on your left for a few yards, then follow the hedge/fence on the left to a gate. Pass through and follow the track to Becca Home Farm. Ignore a track through a gate to the right and the farmyard to the left, and keep forward on the track for about 100 yards to where on the right of the track there is a marker post with a large yellow diamond: here turn left on the path down the middle of the field to another marker visible at the far side.

Cross the bridge and turn left for 20 yards, then go sharp right to a solitary tree, then continue straight forward to the next marker post.

Keep the ditch to your left to reach a stile. Keep the fence and wood to your left, and when the wood ends follow the fence/hedge, soon going right with the hedge to a stile in the next field corner. Bear slightly left across a narrow strip of woodland into the next field, and bear left round the edge with a wood to your left. Pass through a gap in the remains of a facing hedge and keep on by the wood. Near the far corner of this field there is a sleeper bridge and a stile. Now bear half-right diagonally across the field.

Cross the stile and turn right up the road to reach the A64 again. Go left along the verge for about 150 yards, then cross and turn right into a track. When you reach a pylon and a wood, a footpath sign points right over a stile by a gate and a clear path leads along the edge of the wood. You have now entered Bramham Park. Look out for a waymark pointing left down a track between a birch plantation and a conifer plantation. In the dip you cross the infant Bramham Beck. When the wood on the left ends turn right along a cross-track. Shortly after entering another wood keep right at a fork, uphill, but when the ground levels out there is another fork, where you must go left. When you reach an 18th century temple the track bears left and right and you have a view left towards the house. Keep on the track as it winds round, and soon once more you have a wood to your right.

When you reach a T-junction with a white gate to your right go left as directed by the waymark. At the next junction go right, and at the next (possible) fork by a wood keep forward with the wood to your right. Pass through a gate and follow the track towards Wellhill Farm, but keep left at the fork before you reach the farm, soon joining a tarmac access road. You are joined by the main drive to Bramham Park from the left and on your left is the fine house of Bramham Biggin. On reaching the A1 go right, turning left at the entrance to Bowcliffe Hall to cross the A1 by the bridge, then left again on the other side down a tarmac footpath, which leads to the road back into Bramham.

HAZLEWOOD CASTLE AND LEAD CHURCH

WALK 13

8¼ miles (13¼ km); Pathfinder 684, 673. Easy walking on good tracks and paths in the spacious countryside of the limestone belt.

By bus: No. 64/64A from Leeds Infirmary Street to its terminus in Aberford (half-hourly, hourly evenings and Sundays). On Sundays the 56 from Tinshill Silk Mill Drive via Leeds Albion Street and Eastgate is hourly to Aberford.

By car: Park on the main street in Aberford near the north end of the village.

Continue along the road heading away from Aberford, parallel to the A1 over on your right. Pass a pumping station and turn right through an underpass under the A1. At the far side turn right again, then left to walk straight through the yard of Black Horse Farm. Having passed the last of the buildings there is a footpath sign and the track forks: keep left, towards a large pylon and the wood. At the corner of the wood another signpost points left and a narrow path leads diagonally into the wood.

Follow the clear path all the way through Hazel Wood. Wood anemones, ramsons and bluebells carpet the ground in spring, and an occasional patch of primroses has survived. When you reach a T-junction turn left, and soon a stile by a gate leads on to the tarmac access drive to Hazlewood Castle. Turn left along it, keeping straight ahead at a junction, past a gate, to the A64 Leeds to York road. (If there is no stile here, as there should be, then walk back to the junction and turn left along the hotel access road, following it to a T-junction where you turn right and rejoin the route of the walk.) Turn right along the grass verge for 500 yards to the next farm access road on the right, where a bridleway sign points to Hazlewood and Stutton. Follow the track until you reach the entrance gates to Hazlewood Castle (NOT of course along the hotel access road!), where you turn sharp left with the track, ignoring another track forking right a few yards further on. (It is worth having a look into the courtyard of the castle.)

Ignore the next farm access road on the right by a shed, but take the next one by a large sycamore tree, with a sign to Lodge Farm. The track leads straight past Lodge Farm and Newstead Farm, then dips and rises to a T-junction. Bear left here, but in 150 yards turn right again at the next junction, along a track with a ditch and hedge to the left. Top the next rise and drop into the following dip. At the lowest point you will notice a path forking right to a hedge corner: that will be your return route to Aberford. For the time being keep forward along the track. As

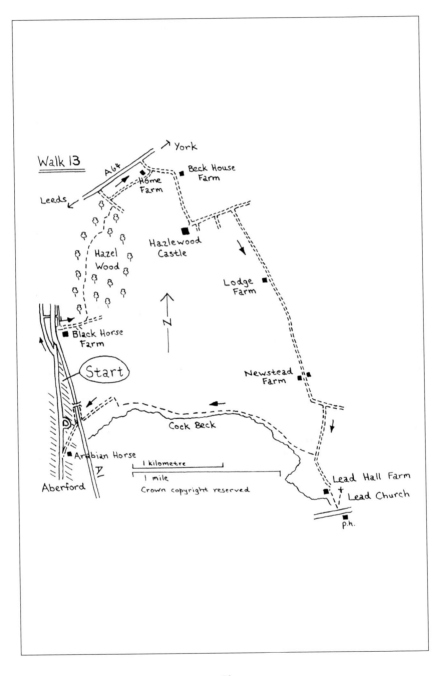

Walk 13

York

A64

Leeds

Home Farm

Beck House Farm

Hazel Wood

Hazlewood Castle

Lodge Farm

N

Black Horse Farm

Start

Newstead Farm

Cock Beck

Arabian Horse

Aberford

1 kilometre

1 mile

Crown copyright reserved

Lead Hall Farm

Lead Church

p.h.

you approach Lead Hall Farm the track becomes enclosed. Follow it to a stile by a gate into a field.

There is no right of way from here to the early 14th-century Lead Church in the middle of the field, so theoretically you must turn right with the hedge/fence to your right and follow it down to a large gate near the bottom corner, from where the right of way makes a beeline back across the field to the church. You may want to take the chance to call in at the Crooked Billet pub a few yards further on.

Now retrace your steps to the junction mentioned above and follow the path down to the hedge corner. Keep the hedge on your left along the edge of the field and soon you have Cock Beck to your left. The delightful path now essentially follows the beck, sometimes close to it, sometimes a little way off. Eventually you pass through a gateway in a facing hedge and now the path bears slightly right away from the beck towards the bottom edge of the wood. Follow the wood along to a stile in the field corner and bear slightly right up to a footpath signpost at a hedge corner.

Cross the stile into scrubland and follow the clear path parallel to the hedge on the right. Eventually the path bears right up the slope to a gateway in the hedge. Keep forward across the field towards a small wood ahead. When you reach it, turn left along the track. On reaching a house on the right, cross straight over its access track, pass to the right of a large pylon and continue along the track to the A1. Here a detour to the right along a fenced path is necessary to enable you to cross the motorway by a new footbridge. On the far side turn left again and at the foot of the slope go right again on the continuation of the track you were on on the other side of the A1. Either follow the track and then the road into Aberford, reaching the main road by a small triangular green and the Arabian Horse pub, or fork right after 50 yards along a short ginnel, then turn right at the street, which leads back to the old A1 by the Royal Oak. Turn right to return to the start of the walk.

SWILLINGTON AND LITTLE PRESTON

WALK 14

6 miles (9½ km); Pathfinder 683, 692. Old tracks and paths, a charming village, and pleasant countryside.

By bus: No. *151, 154, 159, 161 Leeds-Castleford from the Bond Street Centre on Boar Lane in Leeds to Goody Cross Lane, Little Preston (every 20 minutes, at 10, 30 and 50 minutes past the hour, evenings and Sundays half-hourly). Alight close to Hall Road.*

By car: Driving from Leeds towards Selby on the A63, shortly after you are joined by the A6120 Leeds Ring Road, there is a stretch of dual carriageway leading to a large roundabout by the Sainsbury superstore. Turn right here (signposted Oulton) and follow this road (Bullerthorpe Lane) until the Temple Newsam woods start on the right and there is a long narrow layby beside them. Park here, taking care not to block access into the woods, walk along to a track on the opposite side of the road, and start the walk at [*] below.*

From the bus stop walk back a short distance, turn left into Hall Road (a no through road) – you are now on the Leeds Country Way – and follow it down through Little Preston. The road ends at the Hall: fork right here, then bear left on a track round the outside of the Hall grounds. At a cross track with a flight of steps ahead turn right to a large gate and a road. Cross the road to the track opposite, pass a barrier and follow this pleasant new bridleway to the next barrier. Turn right along an old road for 200 yards to find the continuation of the bridleway on the left. Follow this track, which has old causey stones in places, soon along the old boundary wall of Swillington Park. When you are joined by a surfaced track from the left, keep forward along it until a hedged track forks right off it. Follow this for 100 yards to the A642, here leaving the Leeds Country Way.

Cross to the footway opposite and turn right. In 60 yards a footpath sign points through the hedge on the left. The path passes to the left of the gate and follows the fence on the right. Follow the edge of the field until you reach a stile in the far corner. Cross and bear half left over the corner of the field to the hedge opposite and follow this up to the top corner of the field, joining a track on the way, which leads up to a large gate into the farmyard of Gamblethorpe Farm. Before you reach this, pass through two small gates on the right, walk through the yard and follow the farm access road to the main road. Cross over to pass through a gate opposite and turn left along a fenced path.

Follow this path to a stile, cross it, and at a stile on the left turn **right** and follow a line of pylons over grassland. Cross a stile, ignore a barrier by a gate on the left and keep forward under a pylon and along the hedge to the left. Where this ends keep on along the verge, cross straight over a tarmac road and a few yards further on take the access road on the right to Newsam Green Farm. The road becomes a track and leads to a bridge over the M1 (from where there is a fine view left to Temple Newsam House and Leeds city centre).

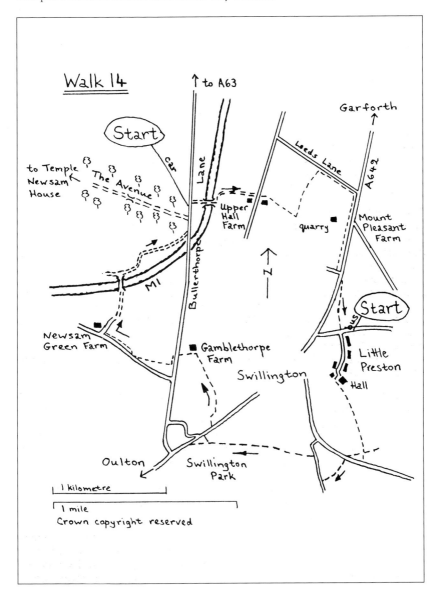

Walk 14

↑ to A63

Garforth ↑

Start

to Temple Newsam House

The Avenue

Leeds Lane

A642

Upper Hall Farm

quarry

Mount Pleasant Farm

Bullerthorpe

M1

N ↑

Start

Newsam Green Farm

Gamblethorpe Farm

Swillington

Little Preston Hall

Oulton

Swillington Park

1 kilometre

1 mile

Crown copyright reserved

49

On the far side of the bridge keep right at the fork and follow the track to Bullerthorpe Lane. Bear left along it. Pass a wide entrance into the Temple Newsam Estate (the house is visible at the far end of The Avenue) and keep on to the end of the footway, where motorists should find their car. If you have come by bus, [*] cross the road and take the track opposite, which soon leads to a bridge over the M1. Then keep straight ahead to the next motor road, Swillington Lane at Hollinthorpe, which you reach through the yard of Upperhall Farm.

Cross the road and take the track opposite, signposted as a public footpath, passing to the left of Hollinthorpe Low Farm. When the track ends at a field fork half-left along a hedged green lane. Soon you are faced by a huge quarry, owned by Swillington Brickworks, which has occasioned an extensive diversion of the footpath. Turn left along the edge of the quarry in a fenced path. Cross a stile into a field and keep forward along the old hedge to a waymark post at the far end of the field, then straight on down the hedged lane to the road (Leeds Lane).

Just before the road there is a bench on the right with a stile behind it: cross this and walk along the lefthand edge of the field parallel to the road. Garforth is over to your left. Cross two stiles and keep forward until beside a road junction the field boundary forces a right turn on you. Continue parallel to the road, now the busy A642. Cross another stile and keep on, now with Mount Pleasant Farm 120 yards to your right. In the next field corner cross a stile onto the farm access road and turn right along it for 20 yards to another stile on the left. Cross this and walk forward along the edge of the field with a fence to your left. Soon you are on a raised bank again parallel to the main road. Cross another stile and at the end of the following field drop down the bank and cross the stile, mounting a few steps to the brickworks access road, thus ending the diversion caused by the quarry!

Turn left to the main road, cross it to the footway opposite and turn right. We are now back on the Leeds Country Way. In 50 yards at a footpath sign on the left fork left into the field and follow a clear path towards the houses of Little Preston, gradually moving away from the road on your right. There should be a tall waymark post to aim for. From the post follow the path along the foot of the bank to a stile, then keep on with a hedge to your left. Cross the next stile and follow the fence on your left to another stile and a road. Those who came by bus will recognise their starting point, motorists will cross straight over into Hall Road and return to the start of the walk description.

GREAT AND LITTLE PRESTON, KIPPAX AND THE RIVER AIRE

WALK 15

7¼ miles (11½ km); Pathfinder 683, 684, 692, 693. Pleasant walking on clear paths and tracks. For ornithologists the wetland area by the river should be particularly rewarding, and for botanists the Townclose Hills SSSI has a wealth of wildflowers.

By bus: No. 151, 154, 159, 161 Leeds-Castleford from the Bond Street Centre on Boar Lane in Leeds to Goody Cross Lane, Little Preston (every 20 minutes, at 10, 30 and 50 minutes past the hour, evenings and Sundays half-hourly). Alight close to Hall Road.

By car: Driving from Garforth to Swillington on the A642 look out for a left fork signposted to Great Preston and Allerton Bywater: this is White House Lane and there is a picnic area 300 yards along it on the right; park here, return to White House Lane, turn right along it and start the walk at [*] below.

On the opposite side of Goody Cross Lane from Hall Road there is a stile: cross it and two more stiles, then keep along the right hand edge of the next field. At its end keep straight forward across the next field, parallel to the A642 on your left, but gradually drawing closer to it. When you reach it, bear right along the footway. Pass the brickworks entrance and, on the right 130 yards further on, just after the first trees, look out for a footpath forking right through the fence. Bear left up the grass to a picnic area and car park. This is where those doing the walk from their car will have parked. Bear right at the car park to reach White House Lane and turn right along it.

[*]You are on the Leeds Country Way. In 90 yards turn left at the footpath signpost, cross the ditch by a footbridge and enter a hedged track. It makes a sharp turn right, then another one left, and reaches the tarmac Brecks Lane over a stile. Turn right and follow it past the large Brecks Farm, ignoring two signposted footpaths on the left. Keep left at a fork. The track drops past Brecks Wood and crosses Kippax Beck before climbing to Kippax. Where the track is crossed by a disused railway line (the Leeds Country Way goes left along it) turn right along it through a large metal barrier.

After a time a few houses on the edge of Kippax can be seen over to the left. The grassy hill half left is Townclose Hills (a Site of Special Scientific Interest), where you will find a plethora of footpaths and in summer a riot of wildflowers. As you reach the hill fork left on a clear path which climbs steeply. Now you must pay attention to route finding! On the way up at a fork keep left. A few yards before you reach the top turn right on a clear cross path, and a little further on fork right on a clear descending path which soon makes for a large pylon in the wood ahead. Pass about 40 yards to the left of the pylon then keep on the contouring path over the grass parallel to the power lines over to your right.

The path leads to a metal barrier and stile in a wooden fence. Cross and walk down the grass towards the car park of Kippax Leisure Centre. Leave the car park to your right and head for the left hand corner of the grass and so reach the road. Turn left along the footway towards the centre of Kippax. The road climbs, and where it bends left you will see on the other side, just beyond Brigshaw Lane, a footpath sign pointing right down a tarmac ginnel. Follow it to the first cross street, where you

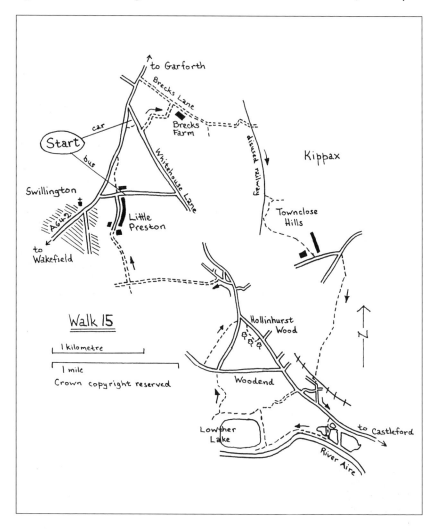

go left for 35 yards to find the continuation of the ginnel on the right. The tarmac surface soon ends, but the path leads forward towards a pylon, passing to the left of it. Follow the clear path until you cross Kippax Beck again by a footbridge. In a few yards keep right at a fork, to follow a hedge on the right up alongside school grounds. The narrow hedged path can be overgrown. The path widens and at the end of the school grounds reaches a cross track. Keep forward on the path which soon leads through a tunnel under a railway to reach a cross track at the back of houses.

Turn left along the track, which soon bears right away from the railway. Ignore side streets to left and right and keep forward to reach a main road. Cross to the footway opposite and turn left. Where two streets on the left join the road at the same point take the signposted footpath on the right. Pass through a kissing-gate and keep forward. The path leads through an attractive wetland area to the floodbank of the River Aire: turn right along it.

Pass through the next kissing-gate and turn right, parallel to the fence on your right. To the left is a large lake popular with anglers. Cross a shallow valley by a wooden footbridge and keep on by the fence. Ignore a gate on the right leading into a fenced path and turn left towards the lake. Pass through a gateway and bear right along the bank of Lowther Lake. Near the far end of the lake turn right up a signposted permissive path between fences and follow the fence on the left to the next road. Turn left along the footway. The road sweeps up in a long right hand curve. Just before it straightens out, cross a stile in the fence on the right, a bridge over a ditch and another stile and walk up the left hand edge of the field.

At the far end of the field cross the stile and follow a none-too-clear path through a young wood to a gate. Turn right a few yards to a road and turn left along it. At the main road turn left again. There is a War Memorial opposite. Ignore Berry Lane on the right, signposted to Kippax and Garforth, and turn into the next street on the left, Whitehouse Crescent. Where it bears right keep forward along Whitehouse Avenue. About 60 yards after this junction take the signposted footpath on the left. When you reach a wooden barrier the path forks: keep right, i.e. straight on, along a clear path. Ignore a path which soon forks right into the wood. When the wood on the right ends, the top of Swillington church tower comes into view half-right.

Follow the path until you reach a junction: on the left here steps lead up the slope to a stile, and ahead the track crosses a concrete bridge over a culvert. Turn right along a broad path with a beck to the left. You have now rejoined the Leeds Country Way. The path becomes a track and leads up along the boundary wall of Little Preston Hall, bearing right round it. At the end of the track, with the Hall on the right, turn left up the road through Little Preston to the T-junction at Goody Cross Lane. (Motorists will now go to the start of the walk description for the route back to their car.)

TEMPLE NEWSAM

WALK 16

4½ miles (7 km); Pathfinder 683. Many hours can be spent exploring the 1200 acre Temple Newsam estate, which contains a wide variety of land-scapes from formal gardens to wild woodland; this walk is just a representa-tive sample. I hope my description can be followed easily, but in the woods there are many paths and path junctions and it is easy to lose the suggested route. The woodland paths can also be extremely muddy after rain.

By bus: No. 83 Leeds-Colton from outside British Home Stores on Boar Lane or the Corn Exchange (every 20 minutes, evenings and Sundays hourly) to stop just past Colton Methodist Church on Meynell Road. Continue down Meynell Road and start the walk at [*]. On Sundays only there is a bus No. 27 from Leeds City Square to Temple Newsam (hourly at 38 minutes past the hour).
By car: Park in the car park near Temple Newsam House.

Make your way past the left hand side of the house to the terrace at the front, from where the countryside through which you will be walking lies spread out before you.

With your back to the House, turn left and at the end of the terrace go down the steps signposted Stable Block. Keep the stables and the Home Farm to your left, where the tarmac drive forks keep left, and when there is a three-way split ignore the cobbled way going through a gate on the left and take the middle drive down through high rhododendrons. Just before you reach the large pond, fork left, leaving the pond down to your right; ignore two paths forking right to cross bridges, but at the next fork keep right, with a car park up to the left. Cross straight over the next cross drive (car park to the left, rose garden to the right) and keep along a valley bottom with the beck to your left.

The track leads through a kissing-gate. At the next junction turn right uphill; at the top of the hill you are joined by another track from the left and soon reach Colton. Eventually the track bears sharp left and reaches a road. Bear right up to the T-junction, then right again. By Colton Methodist Church kink right, then left down Meynell Road. [*] At the bottom of the slope, opposite Woodhall Court, turn right down a signposted footpath between hedges. Cross a wooden footbridge, then straight over a track by stiles into a fenced path which can be overgrown in summer. Cross over another track by stiles and continue along the righthand edge of the field. The path bears half-left to cut the far corner of the field, and re-enters woodland by a kissing-gate.

In a few yards turn left, parallel to the edge of the wood. When the edge of the wood turns right, so too does the path, and where it goes left again, keep with it, ignoring a waymarked path straight ahead and another path to the right. Cross a wide brick bridge and fork left, a few yards further on forking left again into a field. Walk up the righthand edge of the field, and just before you reach the fence at the top, fork right back into the wood and take the clear path away from the corner of the fence through the wood. Ignore cross paths. Eventually your path emerges onto a broad cross track: this is The Avenue, and looking right you will see that it leads directly to the front of the House.

But your route crosses straight over and enters the wood again on a broad path. When you reach a fork, keep left on a narrower path past a marker post (blue route). When you reach a broad cross track, turn right. You are joined by a path from the left at another (blue) marker post, and a yard or two further on fork left on a narrower path (blue marker post). Now you are walking parallel to the edge of the wood over to your left. Just before the path begins to drop quite steeply you reach a couple of old stone steps: fork left here and leave the wood on a path which keeps to the right of a fence.

Cross a stile. There are fields to your left and an area of scrub to the right. The path leads up to another stile. Turn right along the track. There is a fine view to the House and to Leeds city centre in the distance. Follow the track until it bends left (ignore a track forking right here) then right again to cross a bridge over the beck and reach a corner of the wood. Now fork half left off the stony track over the grass to a prominent footpath sign, and turn left along the track. At the next fork you have a choice of routes: for a slightly longer walk, keep left and follow the track until it reaches a stile by a gate a short distance before an underpass under the M1; turn right up the narrow tarmac road and follow it to the top; for a shorter route, keep right, parallel to the fence on the right; just before the track reaches a gate, bear left along to a smaller gate and a bridleway sign. Turn right at the narrow tarmac road. Here the longer variant rejoins you.

Cross the stile beside a large metal gate and walk forward on the tarmac road towards the house. The tarmac goes through a gate and fizzles out, but before the gate bear left along a track with young trees on both sides. When a high hedge begins on the left, pass through it and

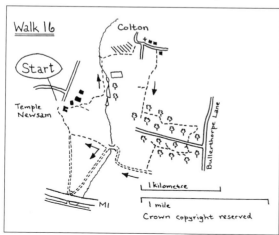

cross diagonally through a formal garden past a small pond. Make your way round the back of the House and through another small formal garden to return to your starting point. Those who came by bus to Colton will now walk to the front of the house and go to the start of the walk description.

55

THE AIRE AND CALDER NAVIGATION

WALK 17

6¼ miles (10 km) to Woodlesford, 11½ miles (18½ km) to Castleford; Pathfinder 683, 692, 693. A surprisingly attractive walk of great variety and much historical and wildlife interest; there is an opportunity to visit the Tetley Brewery Wharf Visitor Centre, The Royal Armouries Museum and the Thwaite Mills Industrial Museum. The walk is of course almost entirely level. Much of the route is part of the Trans Pennine Trail and is waymarked as such.

The walk, which is linear, starts at Leeds Station and the return is by train from either Woodlesford or Castleford (Hallam or Pontefract Lines). It would be possible to leave a car at Woodlesford Station, Woodlesford Lock or in Castleford, take the train to Leeds and walk back to the car.

On emerging from Leeds Station walk straight over the pedestrian crossing to a small white tower building with a sign saying Way Out Bishopgate, go down the steps and turn right, but immediately cross the main road by the pedestrian crossing and turn right to follow the road under the station. Pass the Hilton Hotel, then cross the end of Sovereign Street and continue over Victoria Bridge, then turn left along the riverside path past the Asda headquarters. It leads out onto Water Lane. Pass to the left of the Georgian Old Red Lion (Sam Smith), cross the main roads by the pedestrian crossings and walk straight forward along Dock Street to the right of the old offices of the Aire and Calder Navigation, now the North East Regional Office of British Waterways, noting the triangular red brick Leeds Bridge House, built around 1880.

Bear left along the cobbled Navigation Walk and soon go right along a pavement through a new housing development, which makes effective use of as much of the old warehouses as possible. Ignore a stout wooden footbridge and reach the river bank again. Follow it to the Tetley Brewery Wharf Centre. Keep by the river to Crown Point Bridge, pass under it and follow the broad paved footpath up to turn left over the bridge over the entrance to Clarence Dock, built around 1840, then pass to the left of the Royal Armouries Museum and to the right of Leeds Lock, built in 1822 and still manually operated. Continue on along the riverside path.

Even during building works it should normally be possible to follow the towpath under the South Accommodation Road bridge, but you are forced to leave the towpath just after the large, derelict Hunslet Mill. Walk up the street to the roundabout, turn left to the next roundabout, then left again to return to the canal at Knostrop Flood Lock – you have to walk round a blind arm of the canal to reach it – cross the wooden footbridge and turn right to follow the track between the river and the canal.

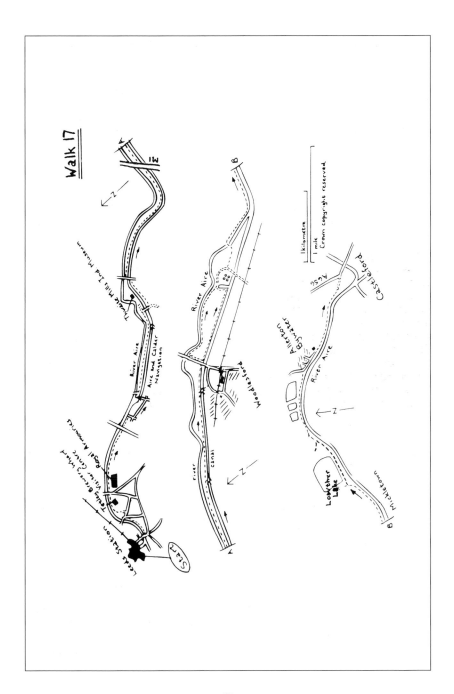

Pass Knostrop Fall Lock by a weir and the remains of a railway bridge, and in a short distance keep right at a fork along a narrower footpath. Look out for a flight of steps on the right (ignore them and keep on along the path if you want to visit Thwaite Mills) leading up to a road, and turn right to cross the canal. When the road curves right turn left to pass through a metal barrier. Soon there is a lovely view over the canal to Thwaite Mills. Pass under the next concrete road bridge and follow the path as it bears right and climbs the steps to the road. Turn right over the bridge, but as soon as you have crossed the canal (and before you cross the river) go through a gate in the white metal railing on the right and descend the steps, there turning right along the path once more between the river and the canal. The next tree-lined section is perhaps the loveliest on the entire route.

After some distance you pass under the new M1 bridge and then under a concrete bridge over the canal. Looking left there is a fine view to Temple Newsam in the distance. Pass Fishpond Lock and follow the path all the way to Woodlesford Lock. If you wish to finish the walk at Woodlesford, cross the canal by the farther set of lock gates and follow the track away from the canal into Woodlesford. Turn right at the next road, ignoring New Farmers Hill, and follow it up and over the railway bridge, then immediately turn left for the station. For Castleford keep on the path with the canal to your right.

Pass under the A642, and continue along by the canal until you are forced left beside a canal basin with oil storage tanks ahead. At the end of this turn right along the track with the river to the left. Pass a high hide and continue along the road. Just round the first bend take the bridleway signposted on the left. At a large tarmac area turn left to cross the river by a new bridge and turn right along the perimeter fence of the opencast coal workings. Keep by this fence, passing two more new bridges (as you approach the second, Ledston Hall is visible half left in the distance) and under a conveyor belt which crosses the river. When the fence turns sharp left, keep with it, and here in front is the old River Aire, which comes to a sudden end at this point.

In about 200 yards fork right off the track towards a footpath sign and continue along the old flood bank of the Aire. The large Lowther Lake is on your left. Pass through a kissing-gate and continue along the flood bank, with extensive wetlands to the left. Soon you join the new cut near its end. Follow the high flood bank until it curves left, then keep forward over a stile and along a lower flood bank. Cross another stile and walk along the river bank to the next facing fence, where a painted arrow directs you left to a gate out onto the road in Allerton Bywater opposite the Victoria Hotel.

Turn right along the road. Along the first street on the left, opposite the telephone kiosk, is another pub, The Anchor. Having passed the line of the old railway, now being planted with trees and landscaped, keep right at the fork, along a road which ends at yet another pub, The Boat. The footpath passes to the right of the pub and becomes a paved path by the river. As one walks along there is another fine view of Ledston Hall to the left. When the paved path ends leave the river and keep forward along the track to the A656.

Keep straight forward into Castleford. Cross the canal and some distance further on Castleford Bridge over the Aire and turn right past The Ship along Aire Street. Opposite Allinson's flour mill cross the road at the traffic lights and walk up to the right of the Job Centre. At the next main road turn right and walk along as far as Powell Street on the left. This leads to the station.

WOODLESFORD AND METHLEY

WALK 18

5½ miles (9 km); Pathfinder 692. Riverside and field paths through surprisingly attractive countryside, including a section of the Leeds Country Way.

By train: Leeds to Woodlesford (Hallam or Pontefract Lines).
By car: park at Woodlesford Station.

Walk through the car park onto the road and turn left downhill to the A642; here turn left again and walk under the railway bridge. Cross the Aire & Calder Navigation, cross the main road as if to join the towpath, but in 2 yards cross the stile on the left (signposted Footpath Link to Leeds Country Way) descend the steps and follow the tarmac path to the next stile. Cross, turn right (here joining the Leeds Country Way) and follow the path to the right of a derelict brick building, then bear right across a stile and walk along the bank of the Aire. Cross another stile and keep forward along a shaly path with a wood to the right. Where this ends, cross another stile and keep forward along the raised floodbank, soon joining a track. Pass to the right of a high wooden hide and follow the tarmac road as it bears right away from the river, with oil tanks to the right. Cross the Aire & Calder Navigation by Fleet Bridge.

Immediately turn left and descend to the towpath. When the track bends right, keep straight on, soon crossing a bridge with a marina on the right. Follow the canal past the lock, then keep straight on past the bollards on a path which leads to a road. Turn left along it for a short distance, then go through the kissing-gate on the left and follow the path between the canal and the railway. About 100 yards before a graceful arched bridge over the canal turn right along a signposted permissive footpath, which passes through a fence and soon reaches a kissing-gate and a road. Turn right to cross the railway at the level crossing. On the other side is The Kingdom pub. Walk along the street, but 100 yards before you reach the A639 take a street on the left which leads past the Royal Oak pub to the main road in Methley.

Keep forward along the road and follow it to where it makes a sharp left-hand bend (there are sports fields to the left). On this bend take the track on the right, just to the right of a derelict brick building, pass round the barrier and in a few yards bear right at the buildings. A faint track continues forward through the fields, keeping a more or less straight line to the next road. It is not well used and can be overgrown. When you reach some trees, keep to the right of them, then forward along the old field boundary, again keeping to the right of bushes and trees, to drop to the road. Turn right. By the Mexboro Arms ignore the road on the right and the main road which bends left, and take the narrower Hungate Lane straight ahead.

Bend left with the road by the entrance to Methley Home Farm, and shortly before it bears left again take the signposted footpath through a barrier on the right and walk up the edge of the field with a wood to the right. The M62 is noticeable over to the left. Keep with the edge of the field, at one point making a sharp right hand turn, until 200 yards after the wood on the right ends look out for a plank bridge over the ditch on the right and a narrow path forward with a hedge to the left. At the far end of the field go right with the field edge and then slightly left again. A few yards further on ignore a stile on the left by a footpath sign. When you reach a small wood projecting into the field, keep to the left of it, to walk down the left hand edge of the wood and into the next field.

Continue down the edge of the field. Now you must pay special attention! About 150 yards from the wood, where the dense hedge on the left thins out, opposite the start of the houses over on the left, find a faint path forking left to cross a ditch by a concrete bridge. Now turn right along the right hand edge of this field. Pass to the left of a footpath sign and redundant stile and follow the field edge down. Oulton Leisure Centre and Oulton Hall appear over to the left. You reach the next road over a plank bridge in the field corner.

Cross the road, go a yard or two right, then left into the field and along with a hedge on your left. About 30 yards before the far corner of this field cross a stile in the fence on the left and bear right down the edge of the next field to cross Oulton Beck by a footbridge. Continue forward to a kissing-gate, then on along the old field boundary (or along a clearer track in the field on the right) to the next road. Cross straight over, passing to the left of the bench on the corner, and take the minor road ahead. About 100 yards along you may like to go through the kissing-gate on the left for a look at a small part of the Forest of Leeds, but the walk continues along the lane until it turns sharp left by some garages. Cross straight over the next main road to return to your starting point.

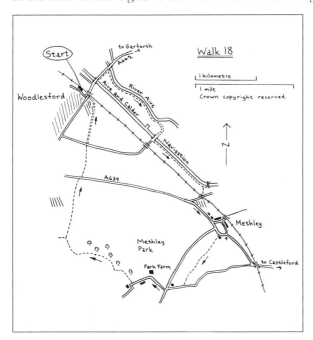

61

AROUND ROTHWELL

WALK 19

3¾ miles (6 km); Pathfinder 692. A mixture of attractive town ginnels and surprisingly rural paths and tracks, the climax of this easy ramble is what is probably the most extensive panorama of any walk in the book.

By bus: 189 Leeds-Wakefield (half-hourly, evenings and Sundays hourly), 410/411 Leeds-Doncaster (every 20 minutes, evenings and Sundays hourly), 445/446/447 Leeds-Wakefield (every 20/40 minutes, evenings and Sundays hourly) from Leeds Central Bus Station to John o' Gaunts on the A639 Leeds to Pontefract road on the northern edge of Rothwell. The bus stop is a short distance before the John o' Gaunts pub, just after the start of the 40 m.p.h. limit. Cross the main road (there is a grass central reservation) and turn left along the pavement.

By car: In the centre of Rothwell, at the bottom of Church Street opposite the entrance into the Parish Church and the White Swan pub, there is a free car park. Park here, walk to the back corner of the car park to a tarmac footpath by the beck which leads to a barrier and start the walk at [*] below.

Cross over the road leading right into the Industrial Estate and follow the signposted tarmac footpath on the right with the high fence of Central Motor Auctions to the left. Where the path ends, cross over the pedestrian crossing by the entrance into CMA to find the continuation of the tarmac path, still with the high fence to the left. In a short distance the path ends and you must keep forward along the street to the next main road. Cross it and turn right. Cross Orchard Way and immediately after the next detached redbrick house on the left turn left down a tarmac ginnel. Shortly after passing a school on the right the path leads into a narrow street.

Keep forward, ignoring Churchfield Road on the right, then St.Christopher's Avenue on the left, but turn right along Gillett Drive. Where it curves right keep straight forward along a hedged footpath, and where it ends at a street keep forward along this to the next road. Cross over and enter the churchyard and follow the paved path to the main entrance to the church (the south porch). Turn left down the paved path to leave the church grounds by the lych-gate (the White Swan is to your left). Turn right to cross the main road to the car park, where motorists will find their cars. In the far corner of the car park a tarmac path with the beck to the left leads to a barrier.

[*] Pass through the barrier into Rothwell Pastures (Information Board) and continue along the grit path parallel to the beck. Soon the scant remains of Rothwell Castle can be seen over the fence on the right. Follow the grit path to a fork, and take the left branch which leads over two footbridges in quick succession. A few yards after the second bridge, at the path junction, take the path on the right parallel to the beck on your right. When the path bears left away from the beck to

another junction, ignore a white footbridge down on the right and walk forward across the grass for a few yards to reach a broad cross path. Turn right along this and follow it to where it ends at a barrier and a road.

Turn right over the bridge and follow the footway towards houses. Immediately beyond the houses on the right, turn right along a broad track and follow it for about 200 yards, then turn left along an unsurfaced track at right angles to the first one. When you reach houses again cross straight over the tarmac street and keep forward along the footway by the track. At the next street, Northfield Place, cross straight over and follow the tarmac path through bollards to reach the disused railway line, now used for a local footpath, the Rothwell Greenway. Turn right along it. In a few yards take the left fork, and 100 yards further on fork left again, on a track which leads to a tarmac footpath on a bend. Walk straight along the tarmac path, and when it turns left, keep forward along the right hand edge of the field, with another disused railway down on the right.

Ignore one track leading across the railway, but at the far end of the railway, when you reach another clear cross track, turn right along it, but in about 30 yards fork left off it down a clear path with an old hedge to the right. Ignore all paths forking left and right and follow the path forward eventually to pass through a barrier by a large gate onto a street. Continue on up the street, and at the main road (Wood Lane) cross diagonally right into a hedged track (bridleway sign). Cross straight over the next street and continue along the clear path. Your route is now as straight as a die all the way to the Leeds Road, sometimes as a path, sometimes a track, and in one place a narrow tarmac road. When the houses are left behind you have a vast panorama to your left, which includes the city centre and Temple Newsam.

Turn right along the footway by the main road. Those returning to Leeds by bus will find the stop opposite the John o' Gaunts pub, motorists will go back to the start of the walk description and continue from there.

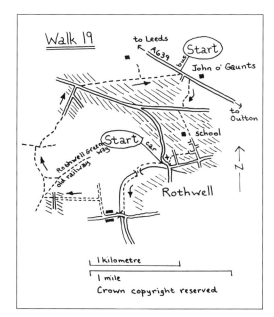

Walk 19

to Leeds

A639

Start

John o' Gaunts

to Oulton

school

Start

car

Rothwell Greenway

old railway

Rothwell

N

1 kilometre

1 mile

Crown copyright reserved

MIDDLETON PARK

WALK 20

3½ miles (5¾ km); Pathfinder 692. Mainly easy woodland walking in one of the major parks of Leeds, and the walk includes a visit to the 15th century Stank Hall Barn.

By bus: 74/74A/74B/75/76 Moor Grange/Horsforth-City Centre (Headrow)-Middleton (frequent service, evenings and Sundays half-hourly) to the entrance to Middleton Park on Town Street, Middleton.
By car: Enter Middleton Park through the main entrance on Town Street, Middleton and immediately fork right to drive down to a large car park on the left. Return on foot to the park entrance.

Enter the Park and immediately fork left along a broad tarmac drive. To your right through the trees is Middleton Golf Course. After a time you have the golf course on both sides and a short distance further along fork right through bollards along a gravel track and soon you reach a hedged enclosure on the left. This is the Rose Garden: when you reach the entrance turn left into it. Diagonally right from this point, in the far corner, is an exit by which you should leave the garden again after looking round it. Pass a bollard, cross straight over a tarmac cross drive, pass a golf course tee and walk down the slope towards the golf course. But before you reach it turn right on a clear path through the trees, cross over a cross path and walk forward on a clear path which passes to the left of another tee into the wood. You reach a major junction of tracks.

Cross over the broad track and then take the second track on the right, descending along a paved hollow way. This is Gipsy Lane. When the paving ends keep forward through the South Leeds Golf Club car park and about 100 yards beyond it turn left off the track by the signpost to Stank Hall Barn. Walk forward with an old hedge and trees to your left to reach rough ground. Continue over this to reach a cross track. The right of way keeps forward over more rough ground to reach the Beeston Park Ring Road down a flight of steps. Cross the road to find a flight of steps up the opposite bank. Up these walk forward with the old hedge to your left, and when you reach a golfers' cross track go slightly left and then continue forward with the old hedge now to your right, crossing several more golfers' cross paths. Now you must pass to the left of some blocks of flats, keeping forward over rough ground with no clear path between the golf course on the left and the fence round the flats on your right.

After a time you reach a clear gap in the fence: go through and follow the path over the grass to the left of the flats to reach a tarmac path and pass through another gap in a fence just to the left. Walk forward over the railway bridge for a view of Stank Hall Barn. Now return over the railway bridge and bear right up the gravel track, with

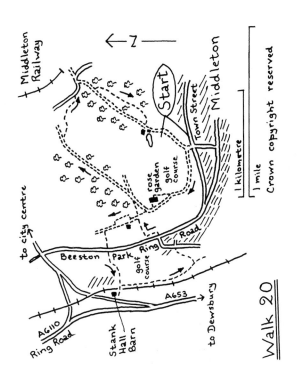

← N —

Middleton Railway

to Middleton

Town Street

Middleton

1 kilometre
1 mile
Crown copyright reserved

Start

rose garden
golf course

to city centre

Beeston Park Ring Road

golf course

A6110
Ring Road

Stank Hall Barn

A653

to Dewsbury

Walk 20

views right to Churwell and Morley. When you reach a junction, the South Leeds Heritage Trail continues to the right, and you might like to explore this path for yourselves, but our walk keeps straight ahead, up towards houses, then bears left and climbs to the barrier onto Bodmin Road. Turn left along this, and soon curve right to reach the Ring Road again. Cross straight over and follow the gravel track opposite. In a few yards a signpost points left to Middleton Park. Where the track curves right, fork left off it along a paved footpath and follow this to the major junction which is already familiar to you.

Walk forward along the broad track through the woods. When you reach a junction of tracks, with a footpath coming down steps on the right, take the left fork and join the route of the former Middleton tramway. Walking on, you are immediately faced by a fork: keep left. Now ignore all cross paths, including another one with a flight of steps on the right, and follow the old tramway down to a junction of tracks with a wooden fence ahead. Here fork right on the track ascending through the wood. The track reaches a grassy area with football pitches. Keep along to the left of these, with the wood on your left. At the T-junction turn left past a barrier to a tarmac road and turn right down this.

The road curves left and descends to double wooden gates. By going left on the track a few yards before the gates you would reach the terminus of the Middleton Railway, but we turn right at this point along a tarmac track to re-enter Middleton Wood through an old gateway. Immediately after the entrance fork left, still on a tarmac drive, but you soon reach a marker post where you fork left over a plank bridge on a narrower path. At a fork keep right, i.e. straight on, ignore minor paths to left and right and shortly after the ground levels out, at a major junction, bear right to reach a broad tarmac cross track. Turn left past a metal barrier. Keep straight on to return to the car park and the main entrance to the Park, but it's worth going right to have a look at the lake, with a children's playground beyond, and calling in at the Lakeside Centre, the modern building behind iron railings, an information centre where leaflets are available.

COLLINGHAM MOOR

WALK 21

4¼ miles (7 km); Pathfinder 672, 673. Quiet, pleasant riverside walking and arable countryside; large duckpond in quiet hamlet.

By bus: 98/99 from Leeds Infirmary Street, half-hourly, hourly on Sundays. Alight at Collingham Memorial Hall and walk along the footway in the Wetherby direction, turning left into Church Lane.

By car: Take the Linton road out of Collingham, and when you reach woodland on the right, find the entrance to a large car park through a wooden arch, just before the road bends left to cross the Wharfe at Linton Bridge. Take the path at the Collingham end of the car park and on reaching Collingham Beck turn right along it. Cross a footbridge and keep forward up the lane away from the beck. The lane bends left. Follow it to the church.

The walk starts at the entrance into the churchyard at the west (tower) end of the church. Follow the path through the churchyard to the left of the church and cross the step-stile into the field. Take the path straight ahead to the next stile, from which the next stile can be seen. Turn right along the bank of the Wharfe with the fence on your right. Cross a footbridge and follow the left hand edge of the next field. At the end keep forward along the river bank. Soon flights of steps lead the path up to the A58.

Turn left along the footway for 120 yards to where a footpath sign points right up the bank. Cross the stile at the top and follow the path up through the wood. Cross another stile at the top and keep forward along the right hand edge of two fields until you meet a cross track coming from Sweep Farm on the left. Wetherby is over to the left and traffic on the A1 can be seen ahead. Turn right along the track and follow it to the A659.

Turn right for a short distance, then take a minor road on the left. After passing a bungalow the road becomes a track and bends right and then left again. At the end of the field on the left turn left off the track and walk up with a hedge on your right. Soon after crossing the brow of the slope there is a wood to your right. Turn right with the edge of the wood. About 50 yards before the end of the wood pass through a gap in a facing hedge and turn sharp left to follow a hedge on your left to a cross track. This is Dalton Lane, the old road from Leeds to Wetherby. Turn right along it. Pass a radio mast and on reaching a fork in the track take the right branch. (A little further along the left fork is Dalton Parlours, the site of a Roman villa, relics from which can be seen in the Yorkshire Museum in York.)

Follow the track to the hamlet of Compton. With the large pond ahead turn right, and at the end of the pond left again, now on a surfaced lane. The lane climbs and bends right. Cross a stile on the right and walk straight through the field to a gap in the hedge at the far end.

Go through the gap and follow the fence on your left down the field. At the bottom cross the stile and keep forward over the next field. Cross the next stile in the corner and a small slab bridge, and head for a stand of conifers. Pass to the right of these and follow the hedge to a minor road.

Cross straight over into a signposted bridleway. In a few yards keep right at the fork, but in another yard or two fork left again between hedges. Ignore paths to right and left and follow the main path down to a street. Turn left to the main road. There is a bus stop a short way along on the left, but car drivers will cross the main road and turn right, and at the far end of the Old Star Inn turn left again. Cross the Harewood Road and walk through the car park of the Half Moon Inn. Pass to the right of a small stone building and enter the Beer Garden. Follow the paved path forward and to the right, leaving the play area by another gate. Follow the ginnel to a tarmac drive, turn right along this, then left at the next road. You are now back on your outward route. Cross the beck by the footbridge and follow the path back to the car park.

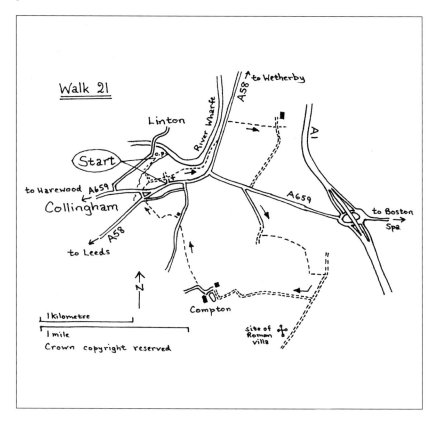

EAST OF WETHERBY

WALK 22

5½ miles (9 km); Pathfinder 673. An attractive stretch of riverside path and easy tracks and paths through pleasant, if flat countryside.

By bus: 98/99 Leeds-Wetherby from Leeds Infirmary Street (half-hourly, hourly evenings and Sundays) or 770 Leeds-Wetherby from Leeds Infirmary Street or City Bus Station (half-hourly, hourly evenings and Sundays). Alight at Wetherby Bus Station, walk back towards the bridge over the Wharfe, cross the road at the T-junction, take the entrance to the car park opposite, and turn right down into the car park.
By car: Park in the Wilderness car park in Wetherby, which is beside the Wharfe near the old bridge (narrow access road).

Walk to the far end of the car park and take the riverside path. This leads past some cliffs and under two road bridges. Go through the kissing-gate and follow the permissive riverside path as far as Wetherby Waste Water Treatment Works, where a track comes in on the left. Take this track, and at the tarmac access road turn left again. At the top of the hill, where a track forks off left, turn sharp right through a gateway (here joining the Ebor Way) and walk straight across the large field. At the far side bear slightly left with a wood on your right and the Wharfe below.

Cross a stile and continue along the right hand edge of the next field. Go through a gateway into the farmyard of Flint Mill Grange and turn left along the access road (here you leave the Ebor Way again). At the next road turn left for 70 yards then go through the small gate by the large gate on the right and along the approach road to Wetherby Racecourse. The road leads to the right of the first buildings at the racecourse. Just past the gate into the racecourse itself keep right at the fork, off the tarmac surface, and follow the track down to pick up a fence on the right. Walk straight over a large car park to reach the Wetherby-York road over a stile by a gate.

Turn right (the verge on the other side of the road is wider), then left along the access road to Swinnow Hill. On reaching a small wood, go through the gate on the left and walk along the right hand edge of the field with the wood on your right. On rounding a bend, Ingmanthorpe Hall can be seen ahead. At the end of the wood keep on along the track. On reaching the tarmac Hall access drive turn left along it, but where it turns left keep forward along a track. When the track forks, keep left, soon passing Sandbeck House. Keep on along the track, but just before you reach a bungalow and a row of stables, go through a gateway on the left and walk up the edge of the field with a hedge on your right.

At the top of the slope cross the stile on the right and turn left along a track. The A1 is below on the right. Shortly after the lane acquires a tarmac surface turn right at the junction and right again at the main road. Cross the bridge over the A1, then take the third road on the left,

Hallfield Lane. The road bends right at the school playing fields. On reaching the phone boxes opposite the cattle market, car drivers will turn left to the fire station, then right to return to the car park, bus walkers will keep the cattle market on their right and take the first street on their right to return to the town centre.

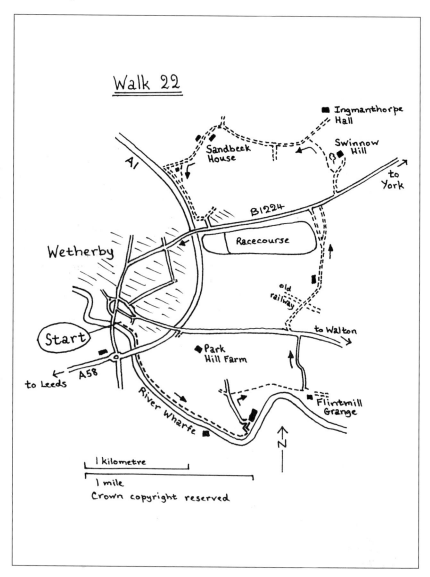

70

BOSTON SPA

WALK 23

7 miles (11¼ km); Pathfinder 673. Fine cliff top and riverside walking, spacious arable countryside, a former spa and a wealth of 18th-century limestone houses.

By bus: No. 770 Leeds-Wetherby from Leeds Infirmary Street or City Bus Station (half-hourly, evenings and Sundays hourly). Alight at the large Parish Church in Boston Spa.
By car: there are free car parks just off the High Street beside the library and along Stables Lane. Return to the High Street and make your way to the large Parish Church.

From the Parish Church walk along the High Street away from the town centre. Turn right along Deepdale Lane. It soon turns sharp left, then sharp right again. On the next sharp left hand bend keep straight forward on a footpath into woodland with a valley on the left. After a time the path bends right and you are high on a cliff with the River Wharfe below on the left. Follow this fine clifftop path until you are almost level with the Parish Church across a field on the right. Here the path forks: take the left hand branch and drop steeply to the river. Thorparch Hall in its park is across the river. Bear right along the riverbank.

At the weir keep along the path on the riverbank. Pass under the bridge linking Boston Spa with Thorp Arch and keep on by the river. On reaching a track keep forward through the gateway into Spa Baths, now private residences. Walk past them and continue along by the river. Having left the town behind, at one point you must go through a kissing-gate and leave the river for a few yards to cross a footbridge over a side beck, before returning to the riverbank. The river bends left and a metal kissing-gate leads into woodland. Here we make a short detour into North Yorkshire. Shortly the path climbs by steps back to the cliff top and to the right there is a factory fence.

Go through another metal kissing-gate and pass under the viaduct of the former Wetherby to Tadcaster railway. Continue along the riverbank. Shortly after passing some islands in the river and two small brick buildings on the far bank cross a stile and turn right away from the river up a fenced track. This is the Rudgate, a Roman road. On reaching the A659 cross straight over and take the minor road opposite. Cross the former railway line by Rudgate Bridge, and at the next junction turn right along a farm access road. On reaching the farm buildings do not bend right with the road, but keep forward along a track. Having passed the farm, cross the stile ahead and keep forward along the right hand edge of the field with ponds to your right. Toulston Hall Farm is further over on the right.

In the far corner of the field cross the stile and turn right along the track towards the farm, but instead of entering the yard turn left off the track and follow a fence/hedge on your right. Keep following the edge of the field until the clear path leads you to the right of the fence and between trees. Here we re-enter Leeds District. When the path leads into another field, keep on along the right hand edge. On reaching the far corner of the field, with Oglethorpe Hall Farm to your right, turn left and follow the hedge/fence on your right. At the next fence corner turn sharp right again, and when you reach a cross track turn right, but in a few yards turn left again. The church tower and houses ahead belong to Clifford, and on the skyline traffic can be seen on the A1.

After a time the track turns sharp left. After 40 yards turn sharp right along another track between two fields. The path becomes enclosed. Where it bends left, cross the stile on the right and follow a fence on your left along. Cross a stile and turn left along another enclosed path which soon turns sharp right and leads to a minor road. Turn left along it. Cross Firgreen Bridge and immediately turn right over the stile and follow the beck on your right along. Cross another three stiles, and now you may have free range pigs to your left (an electric fence protects you from them!). You are now on a track, still with the beck to your right.

The track bends right and then left again, and passes to the left of ponds. Go through a gate and walk through the yard of Low Mill Farm. Turn left along the footway by the A659 to return to Boston Spa, and enjoy the wealth of 18th-century houses you pass as you return to your starting point.

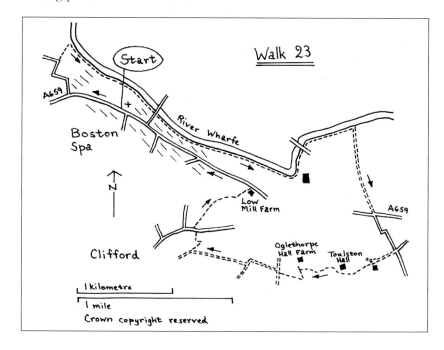

72

LEDSTON AND NEWTON INGS

WALK 24

4¾ miles (7½ km); Pathfinder 693. Good paths through pleasant limestone countryside, at times almost like the Yorkshire Wolds, and a wealth of wetlands, a paradise for bird watchers. The opportunity can also be taken to explore the RSPB's Fairburn Ings Reserve.

By bus: 176 Castleford bus from Leeds Central Bus Station (Mon-Sat at 10.15, 12.15, 14.15), X4 from Leeds Bond Street Centre to Castleford (Mon-Sat at 10.15, 12.15, 17.15, 17.35). Start the walk at [*].

By car: Park in the large RSPB car park at Fairburn Ings, on the road from Fairburn to Allerton Bywater (GR 452 278). Walk along the track signposted "Visitor Reception", past the large information board, and on reaching the information centre turn right through the gate to the road and turn left along it. Opposite the access road to Newton Farm on the right, cross the stile on the left.

Bear half right over the large field, keeping to the left of the ponds and heading for the right hand end of the long grassy spoil heap. Cross the stile by the gate near the field corner and keep heading towards the end of the spoil heap, picking up the fence on the left. Pass through an old hedge and keep along beside the fence. Having passed the end of the spoil heap, there is a large lake on the other side of the fence. The path bears slightly right away from the fence towards some trees. Cross the stile under these and follow the fence on your right. After a time a hedge starts. A board walk made of old sleepers helps you over a wet patch. Pass under power lines and reach a railway viaduct. Don't go under it, but immediately before it turn right.

The path bears slightly right away from the railway and just to the left of a large pylon reaches a track. Turn right along this and follow it to the next road. A short way along a detour can be made to a hide on the right. Turn left along the road. Ignore a minor road to Ledston on the right, and pass the Allerton Bywater Business Park. There is a view right to Ledston, with Ledston Hall above it, and as you approach the next junction, the tower of Kippax church on its hill is prominent half right in the distance. At the traffic lights turn right along the A656 for a few yards, to where a footpath sign points right to a very clear path across the fields.

Follow this path to Ledston and turn left along the village street for about 200 yards. [*] Opposite the bus stop, by the telephone kiosk, turn off the main street up a lane. It soon bends left. Fork right off it into a fenced footpath which climbs past a small wood. Cross the stile at the top, look left for a closer view of Ledston Hall, and walk straight over the enormous field. You are likely to encounter horses on the way. Cross the stile at the far side, cross the track, and keep forward with a hedge on the left. Cross straight over the minor road and walk straight over the next large field, heading for the right hand corner of the nearer wood.

There is a marker post on the far side of this field, but it may not be too easy to spot it.

Keep on across the next field to the corner of the wood, then walk on with the wood on your left. In the corner of the field walk straight through the narrow belt of woodland ahead to the far side and turn left to follow the trees on your left to the road. Turn right along the road for about 220 yards to a footpath sign and stile by a gate on the right. Follow the track through the field, which you leave by a stile beside a gate at the far end. Stay on the track as it climbs to the left of a wood. This is where you might almost be somewhere in the Wolds! Follow the track to Newfield Farm. Cross a stile by a gate into the farmyard and bear right between the buildings to join a concrete track which you follow to the next road.

Cross straight over and take the grassy track opposite between the fields. When you reach the farm buildings, another track comes in from the right. Keep on for a short distance further, but when the track bears right to the farm walk straight ahead down the right hand edge of the field. Cross the stile at the bottom onto the road. Car walkers will turn left to return to the car park, bus walkers wanting to visit the RSPB reserve will also turn left, otherwise they will cross the road to the stile opposite and jump back to the start of the walk description.

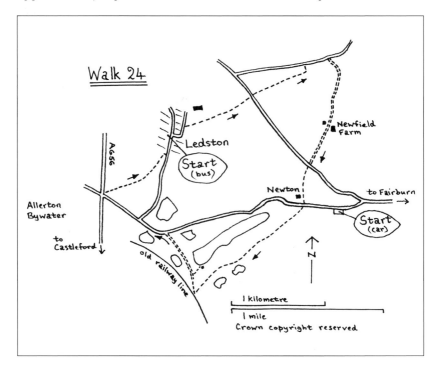

74

TEMPLE NEWSAM TO SKELTON LAKE

5¼ or 7¼ miles (8½ or 11½ km); Pathfinder 683. To a stroll through part of the Temple Newsam estate is added some easy walking over reclaimed colliery land and a visit to a large wetland nature reserve, of great interest to bird watchers. Please note that access around Skelton Lake is at present informal, but this may change due to concern about disturbance to nesting birds. If the path round the lake is blocked off, you will need to retrace your steps to find the continuation of the walk.

By bus: Sundays only. No. 27 from Leeds City Square to Temple Newsam (hourly at 38 minutes past the hour).
By car: Park in the car park near Temple Newsam House.

Make your way past the left hand side of the house to the terrace at the front, from where the countryside through which you will be walking lies spread out before you. With your back to the House, turn left and at the end of the terrace go down the steps signposted Stable Block. Keep the stables and the Home Farm to your left, where the tarmac drive forks keep right, and on reaching the valley bottom bear right over a stone bridge. At the next junction, with a gate and stile ahead and the track crossing a bridge on the right, turn left through the bollards. After a time you pass through two sets of double metal gates and walk forward over the grass to join an ascending path with a wood to the left.

At the top of the slope pause and look back for a view of the house, before walking along the wide Avenue, but only for a few yards, then fork right off it on a clear path into the woods. In a yard or two fork right again, and at the next fork keep left. Follow the path down into the valley bottom, cross the bridge and climb the long flight of steps on the other side. A short distance beyond the top of these there are two stone steps set in the path. Fork right here to the corner of a fence, leaving the woods, and follow the fence along on your left to a stile, then keep by the fence to climb to another stile (there is another fine view right to the house). Turn left along the track, which ends here, and cross the stile on the right, then keep forward with the fence/hedge on your left.

When the fence bends right, keep with it, cross the double stile in the next field corner, and turn left, still following a fence on the left. Cross the next stile and join a track, which soon bends right to cross a bridge over the M1. Look right for a fine view of the house and Leeds city centre. Walk down past Newsam Green Farm and turn right at the T-junction. Take care, as the road past Lawns Farm is narrow and busy. When the road bends right and a footway starts on the right, take the track on the left (there is a large pylon in the field on the left), soon passing through a large gate. Shortly after the high fence on the left is replaced by a low one, the track forks.

Take either branch, as they meet up again later. If you keep left, the track will lead you to a kind of turning circle on the edge of a drop, where there is a piece of concrete with old iron pipes embedded in it. Take the track descending right, and on reaching a cross track, turn left. If you take the right hand branch, you will eventually pass through a metal barrier and reach a junction. Turn left. The two routes have now rejoined.

The track now leads clockwise round a large lake. At the next fork keep left with the main track to the left of a little wood. At the far end of the lake, as the track begins to curve right, an overflow from the Aire and Calder Canal into the River Aire comes into view, with Fishpond Lock to the left of it. The track now passes between the lake and the Aire. After a time the track bends right away from the river again, soon reaching a high metal fence. Keep this on your left. Where it ends, ignore the gate ahead out onto Knowsthorpe Lane and turn right.

Having completed the circuit of the lake, you reach a major track junction. Looking right, you will see your outward route, but this time take the track straight ahead. On reaching the car park, walk straight

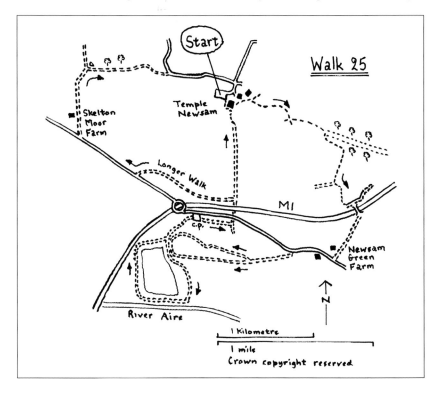

through it and take the fenced track on the other side, parallel to a road (Pontefract Lane). At the next junction turn left, cross the road and pass through the tunnel under the M1. If you would like a slightly longer return route to the start, which does however involve about a kilometre along a busy road, turn left after the underpass and jump to the next paragraph. The direct return keeps straight forward up the old hedged lane. Near the top of the slope pass round the large gate and bear left with the track, then right towards the house. At the end of the tree-lined avenue climb the two short flights of steps to the house and turn left along the terrace. At the corner of the house turn right, and at the next corner turn left to return to the car park.

For the longer walk, having turned left after the underpass, walk uphill on the tarmac road, and follow it all the way to the next motor road, Pontefract Lane again. Here turn right, and take care on this busy road with no footway. Take the first farm access road on the right. Walk straight through the yard of Skelton Moor Farm and continue up the track. At the top of the hill, with a trig point over the fence ahead, turn right and follow the track along the edge of Halton Moor Wood. At the end of the wood the track crosses part of the golf course. On reaching a tarmac road, keep forward along it, but opposite the entrance to a large car park on the left, fork right onto a track, which leads back to your starting point.

Record of Walks Completed

DATE	WALK	START TIME	FINISH TIME	COMMENTS
	1. Harewood Circular			
	2. River Wharfe, Kearby, Woodhall Bridge			
24/8	3. Eccup Reservoir	1 40	3.15	My first walk - with but friend Karol & Kate - very enjoyable SM 24/8/04.
	4. Bardsey, Hetchell Crags and Thorner			
	5. Roundhay Park, Shadwell and Scarcroft			
	6. Barwick in Elmet and Saw Wood			
	7. Barwick in Elmet and Garforth circular			
	8. Barwick in Elmet to Parlington Park			
	9. Kippax to Micklefield and Ledsham			

Record of Walks Completed

DATE	WALK	START TIME	FINISH TIME	COMMENTS
	10. Kippax to Ledsham, Fairburn Ings and Ledston			
	11. Lotherton Hall from Garforth or Aberford			
	12. Bramham Park and Hazlewood Castle			
	13. Hazlewood Castle and Lead Church			
	14. Swillington and Little Preston			
	15. Great Preston, Kippax and the River Aire			
	16. Temple Newsam			
	17. The Aire and Calder Navigation			
	18. Woodlesford and Methley			

Record of Walks Completed

DATE	WALK	START TIME	FINISH TIME	COMMENTS					
	19. Around Rothwell								
	20. Middleton Park								
	21. Collingham Moor								
	22. East of Wetherby								
28/6	23. Boston Spa	3.15	5.30	Lovely walk - Ken was scared of the cows!					
	24. Ledston and Newton Ings								
	25. Temple Newsam to Skelton Lake								